MUSIC IN OUR LIFE

Music IN

IRVIN COOPER ★ ROY E. FREEBURG ★ WARNER IMIG

Consultant in Opera HELEN PLINKIEWISCH

SILVER BURDETT COMPANY

OUR LIFE

HARRIET NORDHOLM ★ RAYMOND RHEA ★ EMILE H. SERPOSS

Illustrated by HOMER HILL

MORRISTOWN, N. J.   CHICAGO   SAN FRANCISCO   DALLAS   ATLANTA

ACKNOWLEDGMENTS

Frederick D. Becker for special material on *Records by the Billion*.

Christie McFall and Merrill Harvey for special diagrams and drawings.

James Dickson, Head, Fine Arts Department, Enoch Pratt Public Library, Baltimore, Maryland, for assistance in research.

Kathryn North and Jean Miller for invaluable suggestions in the preparation of the manuscript.

University of California Press for words and tune of *O, Give Me the Hills*, reprinted from *Songs of the Western Miners* by Duncan Emrich in THE CALIFORNIA FOLKLORE QUARTERLY, Volume 1, Number 3.

Carib Singers for *Panamam Tombê*.

John Church Company for *El Capitan*.

Cooperative Recreation Service, Inc., for *Among the Pines*, © 1956, *Calaloo*, collected by Olcutt Sanders, in AMIGOS CANTANDO, © 1948, *Johnny's My Boy* and *Silver and Gold* from BRIDGE OF SONG, © 1957.

J. Curwen and Sons, Ltd., 24 Berners Street, W.1., London, for words of *German Peasant Dance* by Florence Hoare from FOLK SONGS OF MANY LANDS, Curwen edition 6268.

Daughters of Utah Pioneers for *Handcart Song* from PIONEER SONGS.

Marie Drake and Elinor Dusenbury for *Alaska's Flag*.

Rabbi Jacob Freedman for *Hatikvah*.

Houghton Mifflin Company for words of *Little Joe, the Wrangler* from SONGS OF THE COWBOYS by N. Howard Thorp.

Université Laval, Archives de Folklore, for the tune of *Les Dimanches et les fêtes (On Sunday Afternoon)* in LA CIVILISATION TRADITIONNELLE DES LAVALOIS by Sister Marie-Ursule, published by Presses Universitaires Laval.

Douglas Leechman for *Old Timer's Song* from which *The Day Columbus Landed* was freely adapted.

Desmond MacMahon for *The Kingsway* and *The Merry Gregs*.

W. W. Norton & Company, Inc., for *Blow, Ye Winds* from SONGS OF AMERICAN SAILORMEN by Joanna Colcord, © 1938, W. W. Norton & Company, Inc.

Oxford University Press, London, for the copyrighted words and melody of *Rocking;* and with the estate of the late F. S. Pierpoint for the copyrighted words of *For the Beauty of the Earth*.

Commonwealth of Puerto Rico, Migration Division, Department of Labor, for English lyrics and piano accompaniment of *I Come from the Mountain (Yo Bajo del Monte)*, reprinted from AGUINALDOS DE PUERTO RICO by Miriam Transue.

Silliman University Foundation, Philippines, for *An Ulitawo (The Bachelor)* from VISAYAN FOLK SONGS, collected by Priscilla V. Magdamo.

United Synagogue Commission of Jewish Education for *Who Can Retell? (Mi Y'Malel)* from THE SONGS WE SING, edited by Harry Coopersmith, © 1950, United Synagogue Commission of Jewish Education.

Henri Wehrmann for *Dear Lahyotte (Bel Layot)* from CREOLE SONGS OF THE DEEP SOUTH, © 1946, by Henri Wehrmann.

The music in this book was reproduced from handwritten originals by Maxwell Weaner.

CONTENTS

O, Give Me the Hills

COLORADO FOLK SONG

1

Lyrics (Melody):

1. Oh, give me the hills and the ring of the drills And the rich silver ore in the ground; Where seldom is heard a discouraging word, And many true friends will be found.

2. Oh, give me the steed and the gun that I need To shoot game from my own cabin door; Where Glenwood below where the one lungers go, And we'll camp on the banks of the Grand.

Lyrics (Descant):

1. Give me the hills And the rich ore in the ground; There's no discouraging word, And true friends are found.

2. Give me the gun And I'll shoot game from my door; There's Glenwood below, We'll camp on the Grand.

Handcart Song

SONG OF THE MORMONS

Jubilantly

1. Ye Saints who dwell on Eu-rope's shore, Pre- pare your- selves for man - y more,
For you must cross the rag - ing main Be - fore the prom - ised land you gain,

To leave be - hind your na - tive land, For sure God's judg - ments are at hand.
And with the faith - ful make a start, To cross the plains with your hand-cart.

Refrain — Melody

For some must push and some must pull, As we go march - ing up the hill;

Descant

Push and pull as we go up the hill;

So mer - ri - ly on the way we go Un - til we reach the Val - ley.

So on our way 'til we reach the Val - ley.

2. As on the road the carts are pulled
'Twould very much surprise the world
To see the old and feeble dame
Thus lend a hand to pull the same;
And maidens fair will dance and sing;
Young men more happy than a king.
And children, too, will laugh and play,
Their strength increasing day by day.

3. And long before the valley's gained
We will be met upon the plains
With music sweet and friends so dear
And fresh supplies our heart to cheer.
And then with music and with song
How cheerfully we'll march along
And thank the day we made a start
To cross the plains with our handcart.

Traveler's Song

AMERICAN FOLK SONG

Leisurely

1. I've trav - eled the moun - tains all o - ver _____ And
2. I've crossed ____ the Rock - ies and Cas - cades _____ And
3. I'll mar - ry a rich farm - er's daugh - ter _____ And

now to the val - leys I'll go _____ And live like a pig in the
now I am look - ing a - round_____ For land ___ with - out an - y
live on a farm near the bay. _____ We'll build us a home by the

clo - ver, In sight of huge moun - tains of snow. _____ In
fenc - es In beau - ti - ful Pu - get Sound. _____ In
wa - ter Where the sun sets at close ____ of day. _____ Where the

sight of huge moun-tains of snow. In sight of huge moun-tains of snow. ____
beau - ti - ful Pu - get Sound. In beau - ti - ful Pu - get Sound. __
sun sets at close of day. Where the sun sets at close ____ of day. ____

And live like a pig in the clo-ver, In sight of huge moun-tains of snow. __
For land __ with- out an - y fenc-es, In beau-ti - ful Pu - get Sound. __
We'll build us a home by the wa- terWhere the sun sets at close ____ of day. __

4. I'll grub out the stumps in the winter
   In spring I will plant all I need,
   And then I will wait for the summer
   To grow my potatoes and feed.

5. Of course you've heard of Paul Bunyan
   He looked for a large piece of ground,
   He plowed up the Columbia River
   And dug out the whole Puget Sound.

3

Roll On, Columbia

WORDS AND MUSIC BY WOODY GUTHRIE

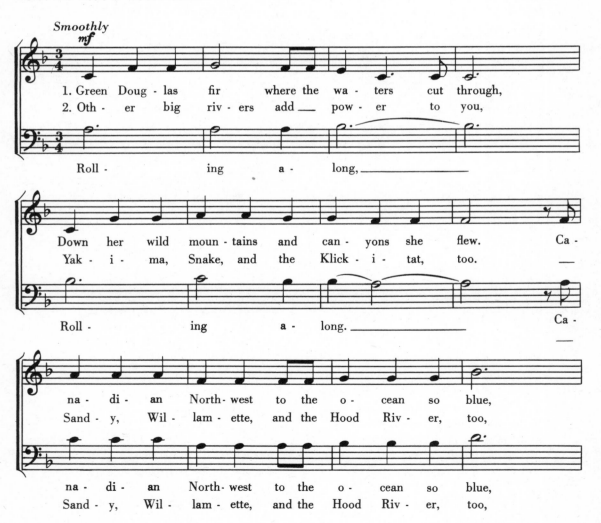

Smoothly
mf

1. Green Doug - las fir where the wa - ters cut through,
2. Oth - er big riv - ers add ___ pow - er to you,

Roll - ing a - long, ___

Down her wild moun - tains and can - yons she flew. Ca-
Yak - i - ma, Snake, and the Klick - i - tat, too.

Roll - ing a - long. ___ Ca-

na - di - an North - west to the o - cean so blue,
Sand - y, Wil - lam - ette, and the Hood Riv - er, too,

na - di - an North - west to the o - cean so blue,
Sand - y, Wil - lam - ette, and the Hood Riv - er, too,

3. At Bonneville now there are ships in the locks,
   The water has risen and covered the rocks,
   Shiploads a-plenty are soon past the docks.

4. And on up the river is the Grand Coulee Dam,
   The biggest thing built by the hand of a man,
   To run the great fact'ries and to water the land.

I Ride an Old Paint

COWBOY SONG

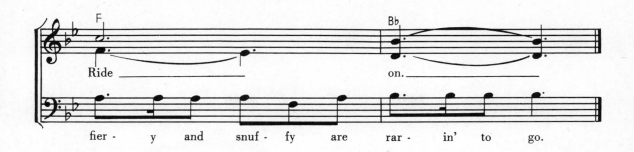

Ride _____ on. _____

fier - y and snuf - fy are rar - in' to go.

Rock Island Line
RAILROAD SONG

Rock Is - land line. _____

I say the Rock Is - land line is a

Rock Is - land line. _____

might - y good line. I say the Rock Is - land line is the line to ride. I say the

Rock Is - land line. _____

Rock Is - land line is a might - y good line. Come and get your tick - et on the

Rock Is - land line. _____

Rock Is - land line. _____

Big Corral

COWBOY SONG

Descant

Hey,   cow - boy,   Press a -

Melody

1. That big   hus - ky brute from the cat - tle   chute,   Press a -
2. The food   we ___ get   ain't ___ fit   to   eat,

long to the big cor - ral,   Hey,

long to the big cor - ral,   He should be ___ brand - ed
                                                  There's rocks in the beans and

cow - boy,   Press a - long   to the big   cor - ral.

on the ___ snoot,   Press a - long   to the big   cor - ral.
sand in the meat,

Refrain
Melody

Press a - long, cow - boy, Press a -
long with a cow - boy yell, Press a - long,
cow - boy, Press a - long to the big cor - ral.

Descant

Rid - in' up the trail, Press a -
long with a cow - boy yell, yip - ee - ay! Rid - in' up the
trail, Press a - long to the big cor - ral.

Sing, Sing Together

TRADITIONAL

I

Sing, sing to - geth - er, Mer - ri - ly, mer - ri - ly sing;

II

Sing, sing to - geth - er, Mer - ri - ly, mer - ri - ly sing;

III

Sing, sing, sing, sing.

Little Joe, the Wrangler

COWBOY BALLAD
WORDS BY N. HOWARD THORP

Briskly

1. Oh,__ Lit - tle Joe, the wran-gler, he'll__ wran-gle nev - er- more, His__
2. He__ said, if we would give him work, he'd do the best he could, Though he

days with the re - mu - da they are o'er,_____ 'Twas a
didn't__ know straight up a - bout a cow; So the

year a - go last A - pril that he rode in - to our camp, Just a
boss he cut him out a mount, and kind - ly put him on, For he

lit - tle Tex - as stray and all a - lone._____ It was
sort - a liked this lit - tle kid some - how._____ He__

Descant

1. Late in the eve - ning when he rode to camp,
5. Joe, the__ Wran- gler will__ wran- gle no more.

Melody

late in the eve - ning when he rode up to our camp, On a
learned to wran - gle hors - es and__ try to know them well, And__

Rid - in' a po - ny he call'd "Chaw,"
Wran - gling_____ days__ now are o'er,

lit - tle Tex - as po - ny he call'd "Chaw,"_____ With his
get them in at day - light if he could;_____ To__

10

Tough look - in' kid,
Spurs and sad - dle,

bro - gan shoes and o - ver - alls, a tough - er look - in' kid You
fol - low the chuck wag - on and ___ al - ways hitch the team, And to

You ne'er be - fore had saw. ___
Bid fare - well to wran - gling Joe. ___

nev - er in your life be - fore had saw. ___
help the co - ci - ne - ro rus - tle wood. ___

3. We had driven to the Pecos, the weather being fine;
We had camped on the southside in a bend;
When a norther came a-blowin', we had doubled up our guard,
For it had taken all of us to hold them in.
Little Joe, the Wrangler, was called out with the rest
Though the kid had scarcely reached the herd,
When the cattle they stampeded, like a hailstorm long they fled,
Then we were all a-ridin' for the lead.

4. Amidst the streaks of lightnin', a horse we could see in the lead,
'Twas Little Joe, the Wrangler, in the lead,
He was ridin' Old Blue Rocket with a slicker o'er his head,
And a-tryin' to check the cattle in their speed.
At last we got them millin' and kind-a quieted down,
And the extra guard back to the wagon went,
But there was one a-missin', and we knew it at a glance,
'Twas our little Texas stray, poor wrangling Joe.

5. The next mornin' just at daybreak, we found where Rocket fell,
Down in a washout, twenty feet below;
And beneath the horse, mashed to a pulp, his spur had rung his knell,
Was our little Texas stray, poor wrangling Joe.
And now Joe, the Wrangler, will wrangle nevermore,
For his wrangling days forever now are o'er;
He has left his spurs and saddle for others here below.
So we bid farewell to little wrangling Joe.

11

Wait for the Wagon

WORDS AND MUSIC BY R. B. BUCKLEY

1. Will you come with me, my Phyl-lis dear, To yon blue moun-tain free?
2. Where the riv-er runs like sil-ver, And the birds they sing so sweet,

Where the blos-soms smell the sweet-est, Come rove a-long with me.
I ___ have a cab-in, Phyl-lis, And some-thing good to eat.

It's ev-'ry Sun-day morn-ing, When I am by your side,
Come, lis-ten to my sto-ry, It will re-lieve my heart,

We'll jump in-to the wag-on And all take a ride.
So jump in-to the wag-on And off we will start.

Refrain

1st time *f* 2nd time *p*

Wait for the wag-on, Wait for the wag-on,

Wait for the wag-on, And we'll all take a ride.

Pretty Saro

KENTUCKY FOLK SONG

Wistfully
mp

1. Down in some lone val - ley in a lone - some place,
2. My love, she won't have me so __ I un - der - stand,

Where the wild birds do whis - tle and their notes do in - crease,
She __ wants a free - hold - er who __ owns house and land;

Fare - well, pret - ty __ Sa - ro, I bid you a - dieu,
I can - not main - tain her with sil - ver and gold,

But I'll dream of pret - ty Sa - ro wher - ev - er I go.

13

Drill, Ye Tarriers, Drill

AMERICAN BALLAD

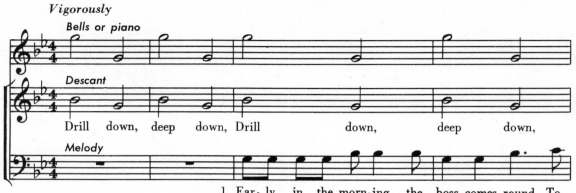

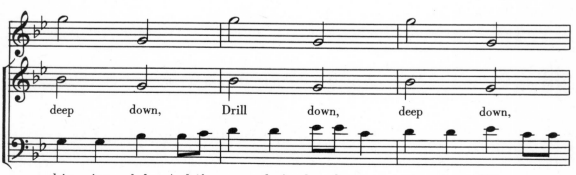

Drill deep down, Then drill, ye tar-ri-ers, drill.

drill, ye tar-ri-ers, drill. Then drill, ye tar-ri-ers, drill.

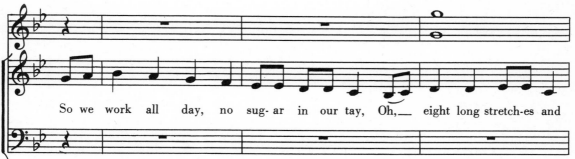

So we work all day, no sug-ar in our tay, Oh,— eight long stretch-es and

six hours' pay, Drill deep down, Drill, deep

So drill, ye tar-ri-ers, drill, So drill, ye tar-ri-ers,

down, Drill, drill, drill. _____

drill, So drill, ye tar-ri-ers, drill. _____

Timber Song

AMERICAN FOLK SONG

Clap hands
Stamp feet

Wal - lace Wade is a tim-ber boss. Woe the day when he gets cross. He

Wal - lace Wade is a tim-ber boss. Woe the day when he gets cross. He

tries his best his men to kill, Say-ing,"Come down heav-y on the old chuck, Bill."

tries his best his men to kill, Say-ing,"Come down heav-y on the old chuck, Bill."

Oh, roll a - way _____ you tim - bers, roll.

Roll _____ you tim - bers, roll. _____ Oh, roll a -

16

Oh, roll a - way _____ you tim - bers roll.

way _____ you tim - bers, roll. _____ Oh, roll and

mf

Roll you here, oh, roll and roll all day _____ No su - gar in your tay,

Roll you here, oh, roll and roll all day _____ No su - gar in your tay,

Softer each time

1, 2

While work - ing on the Wade Boys' roll - way. While

While work - ing on the Wade Boys' roll - way. While

3.

f roll - way. Roll - way, *ff* Roll - way.

roll - way. Roll - way, Roll - way.

17

Amsterdam

CAPSTAN CHANTEY

1. In Am-ster-dam there liv'd a maid, Mark well what I do say, In
2. Her eyes are like two stars so bright, Mark well what I do say, Her
3. Her cheeks are like the rose-buds red, Mark well what I do say, Her
4. And if you'd know this maid-en's name, Mark well what I do say, And

Am-ster-dam there liv'd a maid, And she was nei-ther plain nor staid,
eyes are like two stars so bright, Her face is fair, her step is light,
cheeks are like the rose-buds red, There's gold-en hair up-on her head, } I'll
if you'd know this maid-en's name, Why soon like mine 'twill be the same,

go no more a-rov- in' from you, fair maid.

Refrain

A- rov- in', a-rov- in', Since rov-in's been my ru- in

I'll go no more a-rov- in' from you, fair maid.

18

Good-by, My Lover, Good-by

AMERICAN FOLK SONG

The ship is sail-ing down the bay, Good-by, my lov-er good-by; ___
heart will ev-er-more be true, Good-by, my lov-er good-by; ___

We may not meet for man-y a day, Good-by, my lov-er, good-by! ___ My
Tho' now we sad-ly say a-dieu, Good-by, my lov-er, good-by! ___

Refrain

Bye - low, my ba - by, Bye - low, my ba - by,

Bye - low, my ba - by, Good - by, my lov - er, good - by! _____

2. Then cheer up till we meet again,
   Good-by my lover, good-by;
   I'll try to bear my weary pain,
   Good-by my lover, good-by!
   Tho' far I roam across the sea,
   Good-by my lover, good-by;
   My ev'ry thought of you shall be,
   Good-by my lover, good-by!

19

Blow, Ye Winds

FORECASTLE SONG

Briskly

Piano

1. 'Tis ad-ver-tised in Bos - ton, New York and Buf-fa - lo, Five
2. They send you to New Bed - ford, a fa-mous whal-ing port, And
3. They tell you of the clip-per ships a - sail-ing in and out. And

hun-dred brave A - mer-i - cans a - whal-ing for to go. __
give you to some land __ sharks to board and fit you out. __ } Sing-ing,
say you'll take five hun-dred sperm, be - fore you're six months out. __ }

Refrain
Descant

Ho, high - ho, high - ho, high -

Melody

"Blow, ye winds, in the morn - ing, __ Blow ye winds, high -

Blow ye winds,

ho, Blow winds, high - ho.

ho, Haul a - way your run-ning gear, And blow, ye winds, high- ho."

Blow ye winds, Haul a - way your run-ning gear, Blow ye winds, high - ho.

4. And now we're out to sea, my boys, the wind begins to blow;
   And half the watch is sick on deck, the other half below..

5. The skipper's on the quarter deck a-squinting at the sails,
   When up above, the lookout sights a spouting school of whales.

6. Now lower down the boats, my boys, and after him we'll go.
   But if you get too near his flukes, he'll kick you down below.

7. And now that he is ours, my boys, we'll pull him 'longside,
   Then over with our blubber hooks and rob him of his hide.

Dear Lahyotte

CREOLE FOLK SONG
WORDS BY HENRI WEHRMANN

Leisurely

1. I've trav - el'd round and round a - gain, I found no one like dear Lah - yotte,
2. Bab - bit, my friend, my good old friend, If you should meet her, tell her this:

I've sail'd a - cross the deep blue sea, I found no one like dear Lah - yotte.
I love her more than an - y one, And I will give her an - y - thing.

Refrain

I've sail'd the deep blue sea, I've roam'd a - cross this great big world,

I've nev - er found one so sweet, I found no one like dear Lah - yotte.

Haul on the Bowline

SHORT HAUL CHANTEY

Vigorously

1. Haul on the bow - line, our bul - ly ship's a - roll - ing,
2. Haul on the bow - line, the old man is a - growl - ing,

Haul the bow - line,

22

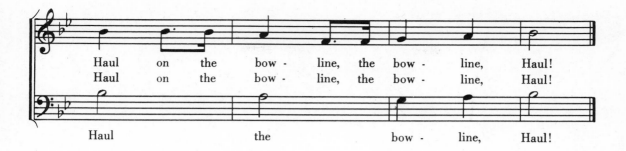

Haul on the bow - line, the bow - line, Haul!
Haul on the bow - line, the bow - line, Haul!

Haul the bow - line, Haul!

3. Haul on the bowline, it's a far cry to payday,

4. Haul on the bowline, so early in the morning.

Paddy Works on the Railroad

RAILROAD SONG

1. In eight - een hun - dred and for - ty - one, I put me cord' - roy breech - es on, I
2. In eight - een hun - dred and for - ty - two, I did not know what I should do, I

put me cord' - roy breech - es on To work up - on the rail - way.
left the auld world for the new, To work up - on the rail - way.

Refrain

Fil - le - me - oo - re - i - re - ay, Fil - le - me - oo - re - i - re - ay,

Fil - le - me - oo - re - i - re - ay, To work up - on the rail - way.

3. In eighteen hundred and forty-three
'Twas then I met sweet Biddy Magee,
And an illygant wife she's been to me
While workin' on the railway.

4. In eighteen hundred and forty-six,
The gang pelted me with stones and bricks,
Oh, I was in an awful fix,
While workin' on the railway.

23

Let Us Break Bread Together

SPIRITUAL

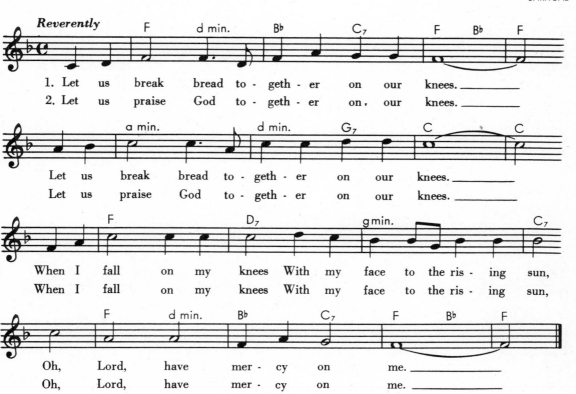

Reverently

F   d min.   Bb   C7   F   Bb   F

1. Let us break bread to - geth - er on our knees._____
2. Let us praise God to - geth - er on, our knees._____

a min.   d min.   G7   C   C

Let us break bread to - geth - er on our knees._____
Let us praise God to - geth - er on our knees._____

F   D7   g min.   C7

When I fall on my knees With my face to the ris - ing sun,
When I fall on my knees With my face to the ris - ing sun,

F   d min.   Bb   C7   F   Bb   F

Oh, Lord, have mer - cy on me._____
Oh, Lord, have mer - cy on me._____

25

Keep in the Middle of the Road

SPIRITUAL

Jubilantly

(Piano)

1. I hear them an - gels call - in' loud,
ain't got time to stop an' talk, Keep in the mid - dle of the
world is full of sin - ful things,

road,
They's a - wait - in' there in a great, big crowd,
'Cause the road is rough an' it's hard to walk,
When your feet get tired, _____ put on your wings,

Keep in the mid - dle of the road.
I can see 'em stand - in' 'roun' the
Gon - na fix my eyes __ on the
When you lay down in __ that __

Hmmm _____

big white gate, We must trav - el a - long __ be - fore it gets too late, For it
gold - en stair, Gon - na keep on a - goin' _____ 'til I get there, 'Cause my
road to die, __ Watch __ them __ an - gels __ in the sky, __

_____ Hmmm _____

26

ain't no use for to sit down and wait,
head is boun' that_ crown for to wear, Keep in the mid-dle of the road.___
Put on your wings and_ get up and fly,

Hmmm _____

Refrain

So chil-dren, keep in the mid-dle of the road, Chil-dren, keep in the

So keep in the mid-dle of the road, Keep in the mid-dle of the

mid-dle of the road, Don't you look to the right, don't you look to the left, jus'

road, Look to the right, Look to the left.

keep in the mid-dle of the mid-dle of the mid-dle of the

Keep in the mid - dle

mid-dle of the mid-dle of the road. 2. Oh I road.
3. Oh the

of the road.

I Want to Climb Up Jacob's Ladder

SPIRITUAL

Jacob's Ladder

SPIRITUAL

Reverently

1. We are climb - ing Ja - cob's lad - der, We are
2. Ev - ery round goes high - er, high - er, Ev - ery

climb - ing Ja - cob's lad - der, We are climb - ing
round goes high - er, high - er, Ev - ery round goes

Ja - cob's lad - der, Sol - diers of the cross.
high - er, high - er, Sol - diers of the cross.

3. Sinner, do you love my Master?

4. If you love Him, why not serve Him?

5. We are climbing higher, higher.

29

Now Let Me Fly

SPIRITUAL

Fly - in', fly - in', up to Zi - on, Fly - in', fly - in', up to

Now let me fly, _____ Now

Zi - on, Fly - in', fly - in', up to Zi - on,

let me fly, _____ Now let me fly _____ in -

Fly - in', fly - in', up to Zi - on, Fly - in', fly - in', fly - in'

to Mount Zi - on, Lord, Lord. ___

to Mount Zi - on, Lord, Lord. ___

1. Way down yon-der in the mid-dle of the field, An - gel work-in' at the
2. I got a moth - er in the Prom - is'd __ Land, Ain't gon-na stop __ 'til I

Oh, Lord, _____ Oh, Lord, _____

char - iot wheel, No so par-tic'-lar 'bout work-in' at the wheel, But I
shake her hand, Not so par-tic'-lar 'bout shak-in' her __ hand, But I

__ Oh, Lord, _____ Oh,

D. C. al fine

just want to see how the char - iot feels.
just want to get up to the Prom - is'd Land.

Lord, _____ Oh, Lord,

Halleluia!

TRADITIONAL

I

Hal - le - lu - ia, Hal - le - lu - ia,

II

A - - men, A - - men.

31

Little Wheel a-Turnin'

AMERICAN FOLK SONG

3. Oh, I feel so very happy in my heart,

4. Oh, I feel just like a-shoutin' in my heart,

Gospel Train

SPIRITUAL

strain - in ev - 'ry nerve. Get on board, lit - tle

strain - in' ev - 'ry nerve. Train is a- com-in' Train is a-com- in'

chil - dren, Get on board, lit - tle

Train is a- com-in' Train is a- com-in' Train is a- com-in' Train is a- com-in'

chil - dren, Get on board, lit - tle

Train is a- com-in' Train is a- com-in' Train is a- com-in' Train is a- com-in'

chil - dren, There's room for man - y - a more.

Train is a- com-in' Train is a- com-in' Room for man - y - a more.

(Piano)

Good Friends, Good Fellow!

FRENCH FOLK SONG

Merrily

Girls — We are good friends, as you can see, **Boys** — Hap-py and full of fun are we,

Girls — Hear us play the

1. cla - ri - nette. / cla - ri - na.
2. fla - geo - lette. / fla - geo - la.
3. ban - jo - nette / ban - jo - na.

Boys — Hear us play the fla - geo - la.

* **Girls** / **Boys**

Cla - cla - cla the cla - ri - nette, cla - cla - cla the cla - ri - na.
Fla - fla - fla the fla - geo - lette, fla - fla - fla, the fla - geo - la.
Ban - ban - ban the ban - jo - nette, ban - ban - ban, the ban - jo - na.

Refrain

Good fel - low, good fel - low, You're no long - er mas - ter in your house When we take o - ver._____

4. tambourette - tamboura
5. cymbalette - cymbala
6. mandolinette - mandolina

7. piccolette - piccola
8. flutinette - flutina
9. pianolette - pianola

10. accordenette - accordena
11. bombardette - bombarda
12. trombonette - trombona

_____ After each new instrument is introduced, all previously mentioned instruments are sung again in reverse order, thus: Verse 2. Fla - fla - fla the flageolet, Fla - fla - fla the flageola; Cla - cla - cla the clarinette, Cla - cla - cla the clarina, etc.

Chumbara

FRENCH-CANADIAN FOLK SONG

2. Fy-do-lee

　　3. Chow-ber-ski

　　　　4. Chug-ah-lee

　　　　　　5. Say-too-mee

　　　　　　　　6. Boom-ta-da

　　　　　　　　　　7. Zow-lee-ski

On Sunday Afternoon

FRENCH-CANADIAN FOLK SONG

1. On Sunday afternoon,____ We take our prom-e-nade,____ To
2. Ma-ma Pic-ard looks up,____ I smile so man-ful-ly,____ she

give the girls the eye,____ As we are stroll-ing by. We
says, "Come in, Re-né,____ And vis-it here with me." Pa-

doff our bright red caps,____ To all the ma-mas near,____ We
pa looks like a storm,____ He frowns so hard at me,____ He

give a wor-ried glance, 'Tis pa-pa that we fear.____ Ma-
knows Ma-ma is boss, And I will get Ma-rie.____ Now

ma Pic-ard is slim,____ Her eyes are like the sea,____ Pa-
Sun-day aft-er-noons,____ We take our prom-e-nade,____ Ma-

pa Pic-ard is stern____ And has no smile for me.____
ma, Re-né, Ma-rie,____ Ma-ma is boss, you see.____

39

Marianina

ITALIAN FOLK SONG

Gaily—not fast

Tambourine

1. Here the south-land sun is warm and bright, Here there
2. She's the one I've ev-er lov'd so dear, That she'll

lives a maid whose smile is bright, In her eyes there shines a
love me true I have no fear, Now I see the pledge in

light so clear, She's the one I love so dear.
her blue eyes, 'Neath the clear blue Tus-can skies.

Refrain

Ma-ri-a-ni-na, tra-la-la.

Ma-ri-a-ni-na, tra-la-la,

Oh, Ma - ria - ni - na, Oh, Ma - ria - ni - na, The stars are

nev - er half so fair as she. Oh, Ma - ria - ni - na, Oh,

Ma - ria - ni - na, the stars are nev - er half so fair as she.

Hunting Song

TRADITIONAL

I   echo

Tra - ra,   tra - ra,   the hunt - ing song,   tra - ra,

II   echo

How   stir - ring and   cheer - ful   the bu - gle sounds,   tra - ra,

III   echo

Tra - ra - ra - tra - ra,   the sound of   the horn,   tra - ra,

IV   echo

The hunt - ing song,   the hunt - ing song,   tra - ra.

41

Funiculi, Funicula

NEAPOLITAN SONG
BY LUIGI DENZA

Some think _____ the world is made for fun and frol - ic, _____
Some think _____ it well to be all mel - an - chol - ic,

_____ And so do I, _____ and so do I!
_____ To pine and sigh, _____ to pine and sigh; _____

But I, _____ I love to spend my time in sing- ing Some joy-oussong, _____

_____ some joy- ous song; _____ To set _____ the air with mu-sic brave-ly

ring - ing _____ Is far from wrong, _____ is far from wrong! _____

la la la la

42

Harken! Harken! Music sounds afar!

La, la la la la La, la la la la La, la la la la La, la la la la

Harken! Harken! Music sounds afar! Fu-ni-cu-

La, la la la la La, la la la la La, la la la la la,

crescendo

li, fu-ni-cu-la, fu-ni-cu-li, fu-ni-cu-la!

La, la, la, la!

f

Joy is ev-'ry-where, Fu-ni-cu-li, fu-ni-cu-la! Hey!

La Cloche

FRENCH FOLK SONG

I
f Din, Din, din, din, C'est la clo-che du ma-tin
p Don, Don, don, don, C'est la voix du gros bour-don

II

III
Qui sonn' au re-tour du jour Bon-jour! Bon-jour!
Qui chan-te quand vient le soir Bon-soir! Bon-soir!

IV

Santa Lucia

NEAPOLITAN FOLK SONG

44

ci - a, San - ta Lu - ci - a. San - ta Lu - ci - a.
ci - a, San - ta Lu - ci - a. San - ta Lu - ci - a.
ci - a! San - ta Lu - ci - a. San - ta Lu - ci - a.

The Appenzeller

SWISS FOLK SONG
TRANSLATION BY HELEN PLINKIEWISCH

1. My fa - ther comes from Ap - pen - zell,
2. My fa - ther is a hand-some man, Dee - ah - lah - oo, dee - ah - lah - oo, doo - lee - ho.
3. My fa - ther comes from Ap - pen - zell,

He keeps no wine, or so they tell.
Wears Sun - day pants when - e'er he can. Dee - ah - lah - oo, dee - ah - lah - oo, ho.
He eats both cheese and plate, as well.

5. My mother makes a happy home,
Because of that I never roam.

6. When others travel far and wide,
They soon return and here reside.

7. The prettiest girls, you understand,
Are found right here in Switzerland!

Holla Hi, Holla Ho!

BAVARIAN FOLK SONG
TRANSLATION BY HELEN PLINKIEWISCH

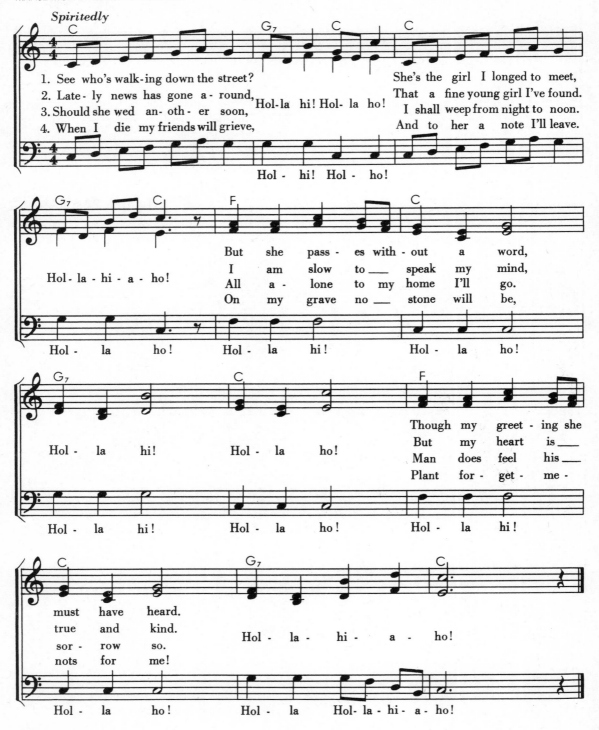

1. See who's walk-ing down the street? She's the girl I longed to meet,
2. Late-ly news has gone a-round, Hol-la hi! Hol-la ho! That a fine young girl I've found.
3. Should she wed an-oth-er soon, I shall weep from night to noon.
4. When I die my friends will grieve, And to her a note I'll leave.

Hol- hi! Hol- ho!

Hol- la - hi - a - ho!

But she pass-es with-out a word,
I am slow to ___ speak my mind,
All a-lone to my home I'll go.
On my grave no ___ stone will be,

Hol- la ho! Hol- la hi! Hol- la ho!

Hol- la hi! Hol- la ho!

Though my greet-ing she
But my heart is ___
Man does feel his ___
Plant for-get- me -

Hol- la hi! Hol- la ho! Hol- la hi!

must have heard.
true and kind.
sor- row so. Hol- la - hi - a - ho!
nots for me!

Hol- la ho! Hol- la Hol- la-hi-a-ho!

The Farmer's Boy

SWISS FOLK SONG
TRANSLATION BY HELEN PLINKIEWISCH

1. The farm - er's boy, he likes to say, "Hel - lo" and "how are you to - day?" The farm - er's boy, he likes to say, "Hel - lo" and "how are you?" Fi - di - ri, fi - di - ra, fi - di - ra - la la, Fi - di - ra - la la, fi - di - ra - la - la. The farm - er's boy, he likes to say, "Hel - lo" and "how are you?" The farm - er's boy, he likes to say, "Hel - lo" and "how are you?"

2. He is a strong and hand - some lad, The best the farm - er ev - er had. He is a strong and hand - some lad, He works the fields all day. Fi - di - ri, fi - ra - la la, Fi - di - ra - la, ra - la - la. He is a strong and hand - some lad, He works the fields all day. He is a strong and hand - some lad, He works the fields all day.

3. With girls he never seems to be
As jolly as he is with me.
With girls he always seems to be
Too bashful and too shy.

4. Perhaps he'll always be alone
Without his true and only one.
Perhaps he'll always be alone
Until his life is done.

47

German Peasants' Dance

WÜRTTEMBERG FOLK SONG

Brightly

mf

1. Leave lag-gards to their dream-ing, Let i-dlers mope at will,
2. Be loth to lose a min-ute When each can glad-ness bring,
3. Our hearts to pleas-ure warm-ing, We'll drain each bliss-ful hour.

1. Leave lag-gards to their dream-ing, Let i-dlers mope at will,
2. Be loth to lose a min-ute When each can glad-ness bring,
3. Our hearts to pleas-ure warm-ing, We'll drain each bliss-ful hour.

The sun-girt world is gleam-ing, And May is o'er the hill.
The red-wing and the lin-net Are two long hours a-wing.
As bus-y in-sects swarm-ing Sip deep the bloom-ing flower.

The sun-girt world is gleam-ing, And May is o'er the hill.
The red-wing and the lin-net Are two long hours a-wing.
As bus-y in-sects swarm-ing Sip deep the bloom-ing flower.

The fid-dler boys have come To tune it mer-ri-ly,
Nor wait to choose your best Of silk or bod-ice blue;
Your heart beats glad as mine To ev-'ry song of May,

The fid-dler boys have come To tune it mer-ri-ly,
Nor wait to choose your best Of silk or bod-ice blue;
Your heart beats glad as mine To ev-'ry song of May,

48

And ev - 'ry beat they're strum - ming, You're pledged _ to dance _ with me.
The fields are dressed so gai - ly, That none _ will look _ at you.
Till time o'er - takes our foot - steps We'll dance _ the hours _ a - way.

And ev - 'ry beat they're strum - ming, You're pledged to dance with me.
The fields are dressed so gai - ly, That none will look at you.
Till time o'er - takes our foot - steps We'll dance the hours a - way.

B♭ Trumpets

Trombones

49

Korobushka

RUSSIAN FOLK SONG

With a steady beat

1. Full to the brim is my fine ko - ro - bush - ka Packed with
2. Here are my goods, they have cost much mon - ey, ___ Come and
3. I shall be wait - ing by yon - der road - way, ___ There to

Pom, pom, pom, pom, pom, pom, pom, pom, Pom, pom,

cot - ton, silk, and lace; I am young and ___ strong and
see my bar - gains fine; Look, young maid, at the goods I
stay 'til dusk shall fall; Then to you, my dear maid, I

pom, pom, pom, pom, pom, my dear one, Pom, pom, pom, pom, pom, pom

stur - dy, ___ With my knap - sack on my back. I am
of - fer, ___ Come and sit be - neath the pines. Look, young
of - fer, ___ Silks and lac - es, one and all. Then to

pom, pom, Pom, pom, pom, pom, pom, pom, pom, my dear one, Pom, pom,

young and ___ strong and stur - dy, ___ With my knap - sack on my back.
maid, at the goods I of - fer, ___ Come and sit be - neath the pines.
you, my dear maid, I of - fer, ___ Silks and lac - es, one and all.

pom, pom, pom, pom, pom, pom, Pom, pom, pom, pom, pom, pom, pom.

50

The Bachelor

PHILIPPINE FOLK SONG
TRANSLATION BY KATHRYN JACKSON

Aloha Oe

MUSIC BY QUEEN LILIUOKALANI
TRANSLATION BY CHARLES E. KING

1. Proud-ly sweeps the rain cloud by the cliffs _____ As
2. Thus sweet mem-o-ries come back to me, _____ Bringing
1. Ha - a - heo e ka u - a i na pa - li Ke

Hmmm _____ _____

on-ward it glides through the trees; _____ It _____ seems to be fol-low-ing the
fresh re-mem-brance of the past; _____ Dear-est one, yes, _____ thou _____ art mine
ni - hi a - e la i ka - na - he - le E u hai a - na pa - ha i ka

Hmmm _____ Hmmm _____

52

li - ko, The _ a - hi - hi - le - hu - a of the vale. _
own, _ From the true love shall nev - er de - part. _
li - ko Pu - a a - hi - hi - le - hu - a o _ u - ka.

Hmmm

Refrain (Unaccompanied)

Fare - well to thee, fare - well to thee, Thou charm - ing one who dwells a - mong the
A - lo - ha oe, a - lo - ha oe, E ke o - na o - na no - ho i ka

Hmmm

bow - ers; One fond em - brace be - fore I now de - part, Un - til we meet _ a - gain.
li - po; One fond em - brace a ho - i a - e a - u, Un - til we meet _ a - gain. _

Hmmm   Hmmm   Hmmm _

Alternate refrain

Bells or voices   Hmmm   Hmmm Hmmm

Fare - well to thee, fare - well to thee, Thou charm - ing one who dwells a - mong the
A - lo - ha oe, a - lo - ha oe, E ke o - na o - na no - ho i ka

Hmmm _   Hmmm   Hmmm Hmmm   _

bow - ers; One fond em - brace be - fore I now de - part, Un - til we meet _ a - gain. _
li - po; One fond em - brace a ho - i a - e a - u, Un - til we meet _ a - gain.

Sakura

JAPANESE FOLK SONG
TRANSLATION BY LORENE HOYT

1. Sa-ku-ra, Sa-ku-ra, Cher-ry blos-soms ev-'ry-where. Clouds of glo-ry fill the sky, Mist of beau-ty in the air, Love-ly col-ors float-ing by, Sa-ku-ra, Sa-ku-ra Let all come sing- ing.

2. Sa-ku-ra, Sa-ku-ra, Blos-soms wav-ing in the breeze. Yo-shi-no, the cher-ry land, Tat-su-ta, the ma-ple trees, Ka-ra-sa-ki, pine tree grand, Sa-ku-ra, Sa-ku-ra Let all come sing- ing.

Sa-ku-ra, Sa-ku-ra, Yo-yo-gi no so-ra wa, Mi-wa-ta-su ka-gi-ri. Ka-su-mi ka ku-mo-ka, Ni-o-i zo i-zu-ru I-za-ya, i-za-ya mi ni yu kan.

54

Among the Pines

ASSAM FOLK SONG
TRANSLATION BY MAX V. EXNER

1. A - mong the pines that bend their fra - grant boughs, The for - est
2. Ah, Tiew - la - run, my own be - lov - ed flow'r, To you, a -

winds their whis-pered tales un - fold; The splen-did stars like jew - els light the
lone, my heart is ev - er drawn; By day and night my eyes see you a -

sky, And now the moon has turned the wa - ters gold.
lone, You are my day, my night, my ris - ing dawn.

Refrain

Descant

Ah, Tiew-la - run, * flow'r of mine, Ooh _____

Melody

Ah, Tiew-la - run, be - lov-ed flow'r of mine, When will you come? I ask the si - lent

Tiew - la - run, Tiew - la - run. _____

pine. _____ Ah, Tiew-la - run, Ah, Tiew - la - run. _____

*Girl's name, pronounced *Taû' - lä - rŏon'*

55

Hatikvah

TRADITIONAL HEBREW MELODY
TRANSLATION BY RABBI JACOB FREEDMAN

Vigorously

Prom-ised land of Zi - on Where he - roes lived and died! Mar - tyred, thy

Prom - ised land where he - roes died! Mar - tyred, thy

chil - dren, Stir with hope and pride! From dis - tant lands of ex - ile to

chil - dren, Stir with pride! From dis - tant lands to

bless- ed East- ern shore, Zi - on, thy faith - ful stream for-ev - er more!

East - ern shore, Zi - on, thy faith - ful, ev - er more!

Refrain

Nev - er! Nev - er! Will our hope be lost! Land of Is - rael

Nev - er! Nev - er! Will our hope be lost! Land of Is - rael

Held in sa - cred trust! Turn to our own land, to the land of Is - ra - el!

Sa - cred trust! Turn to our own land, land of Is - rael!

56

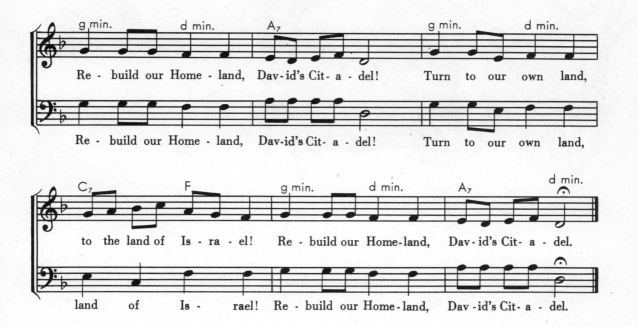

g min.   d min.   A₇   g min.   d min.

Re - build our Home - land, Dav-id's Cit- a - del! Turn to our own land,

Re - build our Home - land, Dav-id's Cit- a - del! Turn to our own land,

C₇   F   g min.   d min.   A₇   d min.

to the land of Is - ra - el! Re - build our Home-land, Dav-id's Cit- a - del.

land of Is - rael! Re - build our Home - land, Dav-id's Cit- a - del.

Make New Friends

TRADITIONAL ROUND

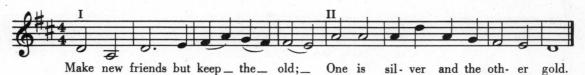

Make new friends but keep _ the _ old; _ One is sil - ver and the oth- er gold.

Who Comes Laughing

TRADITIONAL ROUND

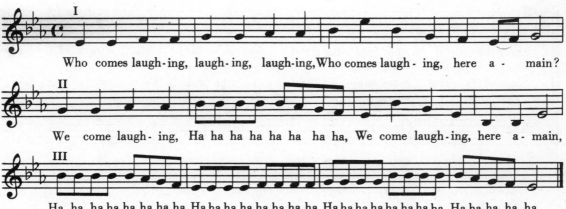

Who comes laugh-ing, laugh-ing, laugh-ing, Who comes laugh-ing, here a - main?

We come laugh-ing, Ha ha ha ha ha ha ha ha, We come laugh-ing, here a - main,

Ha ha ha ha ha ha ha ha, Ha ha ha ha ha ha ha ha, Ha ha ha ha ha ha ha ha, Ha ha ha ha ha.

57

The Ash Grove

WELSH FOLK SONG
WORDS BY JOHN OXENFORD

Violin, flute or bells

1. The ash grove, how graceful, how plainly 'tis speaking, The
   When over its branches, the sunlight is breaking, A
2. My laughter is over, my step loses lightness, Old
   I only remember the past and its brightness; The

1. Ash grove graceful plain 'tis speaking,
   O-ver branch-es, light is break-ing,
2. Laugh-ter o-ver, step los-es light,____
   I re-mem-ber past so bright,____

harp through it playing has language for me. The friends of my
host of kind faces is gazing on me.
coun-try-side measures steal soft on my ear; From ev-'ry dark
dear ones I mourn for again gather here.

Harp play-ing for_____ me. My_____
Host of fac-es gazing on me.
Coun-try meas-ures soft on my heart. They_____
Ones I mourn for gath-er here.

58

child-hood a - gain are _ be - fore me, Each step wakes_ a _ mem - 'ry, as
nook they press for - ward_ to _ meet me, I lift up_ my _ eyes to the

_ child - hood a- gain, _____ Each_ step_ wakes a mem - 'ry
_ press_t'ward _ me _____ I _ lift _ my _____ eyes to

free - ly I roam. With soft whis- pers lad - en, its leaves rus - tle_
broad leaf - y dome; And oth - ers are_ there, look - ing down-ward_ to _

free - ly I roam. Whis - pers lad - en leaves
yon leaf - y dome; Oth - ers there look down to

o'er me; The ash grove,_ the _ ash grove a - lone is my home.
greet me; The ash grove,_ the _ ash grove a - lone is my home.

rus - tle, Ash grove, ash grove is my home.
greet me, Ash grove, ash grove is my home.

The Minstrel Boy

IRISH FOLK SONG
WORDS BY THOMAS MOORE

1. The min-strel boy __ to the war is gone, In the ranks of death __ you'll find him; His fa-ther's sword __ he has gird - ed on, And his wild harp slung __ be-hind him. __ "Land of song!" said the war - rior bard, "Though all the world be-trays __ thee, One sword, at least, __ thy __ rights shall guard, One __ faith - ful harp __ shall praise thee."

2. The min-strel fell, __ but the foe - man's chain Could not bring that proud __ soul un - der; The harp he loved __ ne'er __ spoke a - gain, For he tore its chords __ a - sun - der; And said, "No chain shall __ sul - ly thee, Thou soul of love and brav - er - y! Thy songs were made __ for the pure and free, They shall nev - er sound __ in slav - 'ry."

All Through the Night

WELSH FOLK SONG

The Merry Gregs

ENGLISH GLEE

1. Let po - ets and his - to - ri - ans re -
2. If in - no - cent va - ri - e - ty, con -

cord ye brave Gre - go - ri - ans In long and_ mer - ry songs.
tent and sweet so - ci - e - ty, Can make us_ mor - tals blest.

While hearts and voic - es join - ing, In glad - some songs com - bin - ing,
In fel - low - ship u - ni - ted, With har - mo - ny de - light - ed,

Sing forth their death - less_ praise,_ Sing forth their_ death - less_ praise.
We em - u - late the_ best,_ We em - u - late the_ best.

This Happy Song

TRADITIONAL ROUND

This hap - py song To you I bring, With all my heart To you I sing.

62

The Kingsway

SCANDINAVIAN FOLK MELODY
WORDS BY DESMOND MacMAHON

With a martial air

Hear the tramp of sol - diers, Ring - ing on the Kings - way,

Swing - ing on the Kings-way as we march a - long. Hear the sound of voic - es

Cry - ing on the Kings - way, Ris - ing on the Kings - way from a

hun - dred strong. Men shall tell our sto - ry when the years have passed.

Vic - to - ry our glo - ry while the earth shall last. Men shall tell our sto - ry when the

years have passed. Vic - to - ry our glo - ry while the earth shall last.

Johnny's My Boy

GHANA FOLK SONG
COUNTER MELODIES BY MAX V. EXNER

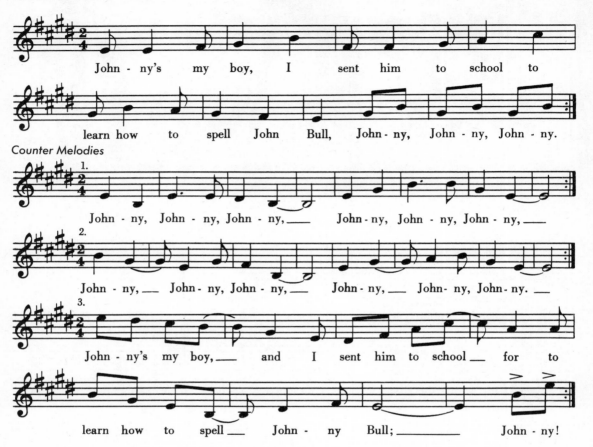

Johny's my boy, I sent him to school to
learn how to spell John Bull, John - ny, John - ny, John - ny.

Counter Melodies

1.
John - ny, John - ny, John - ny, ___ John - ny, John - ny, John - ny, ___

2.
John - ny, ___ John - ny, John - ny, ___ John - ny, ___ John - ny, John - ny. ___

3.
John - ny's my boy, ___ and I sent him to school ___ for to
learn how to spell ___ John - ny Bull; _____ John - ny!

Calaloo

ST. CROIX FOLK SONG

Joyously

Flute

Hmmm ca - la - loo, Hmmm ca - la - loo,

Ev - 'ry day is ca - la - loo. Ev - 'ry day is ca - la - loo.

The Charcoal Man

MEXICAN FOLK TUNE

Gaily

1. The ver-y first sweet-heart I've had,__ Mam-ma, Has to work__ at char-coal

burn-ing; He has to go sell-ing his coals,__ Mam-ma, But

Descant—Girls

Car-men has a sweet-heart,

brave-ly he spends all he's earn-ing. 2. Ah, yon-der he comes, my

Car-men has a sweet-heart, Car-men tie-ne

coal-man, Mam-ma,__ De-scend-ing the ridge at his lei-sure; He's

no-vio, si Car-men tie-ne

sell-ing the char-coal he made,__ Mam-ma, At a dime and a half the pint

66

no - vio. Si si _____ si si, _____ I

meas - ure. 3. Ah, yon - der he comes, my coal - man, Mam - ma, ___

Descant—Boys

Si si _____ si si, _____

see _____ her lov - er. Si si _____ si

Com - ing on down by the sta - ble; He's go - ing to shake out the

___ I see _____ her lov - er. Si si _____

si, _____ Se ve _____ su no - vio.

char - coal, Mam - ma, But saves ___ the sacks when he's a - ble.

___ si si, _____ Se ve _____ su no - vio.

Kling klang, kling klang, rings the

4. I'm go - ing to build me a chap - el, Mam - ma, ___ Of peb - bles the ants un -

Kling klang, kling klang, rings the

Panamam Tombé

CALYPSO SONG

Rhythm Pattern for Latin American Songs

Claves

Maracas
Guiro

Cowbell

Conga
drum

Bongo

How Firm a Foundation

"K" IN RIPPON'S *A SELECTION OF HYMNS*

With spirit and dignity

1. How firm a foun-da-tion, ye saints of the Lord,
2. Fear not, I am with thee, O be not dis-mayed,
3. When through the deep wa-ters I call thee to go,
4. The soul that on Je-sus still leans for re-pose,

Is laid for your faith in His ex-cel-lent word!
For I am thy God, and will still give thee aid;
The riv-ers of woe shall not thee o-ver-flow;
I will not, I will not de-sert to His foes;

What more can He say than to you He hath said,
I'll strength-en thee, help thee, and cause thee to stand,
For I will be with thee thy trou-bles to bless,
That soul, though all hell should en-deav-or to shake,

To you who for ref-uge to Je-sus have fled?
Up-held by My right-eous, om-nip-o-tent hand.
And sanc-ti-fy to thee thy deep-est dis-tress.
I'll nev-er, no, nev-er, no, nev-er for-sake!

Simple Gifts

SHAKER HYMN

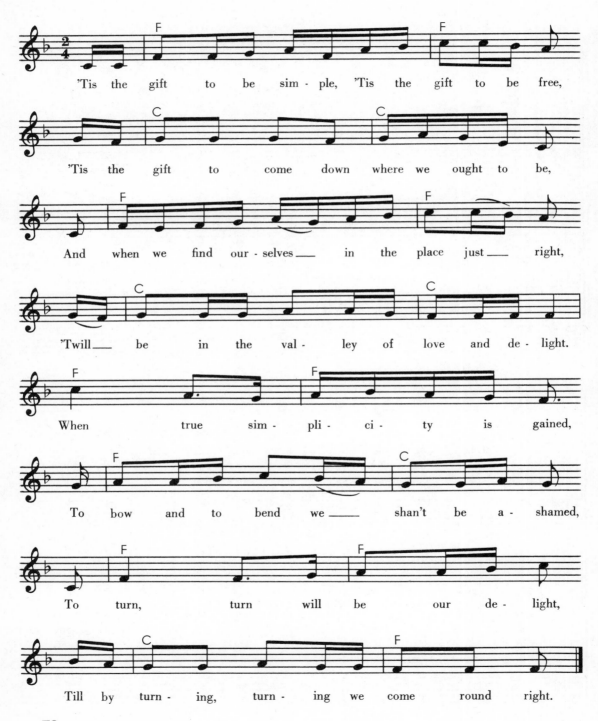

'Tis the gift to be sim - ple, 'Tis the gift to be free,

'Tis the gift to come down where we ought to be,

And when we find our - selves ___ in the place just ___ right,

'Twill ___ be in the val - ley of love and de - light.

When true sim - pli - ci - ty is gained,

To bow and to bend we ___ shan't be a - shamed,

To turn, turn will be our de - light,

Till by turn - ing, turn - ing we come round right.

Amazing Grace

EARLY AMERICAN MELODY
WORDS BY JOHN NEWTON

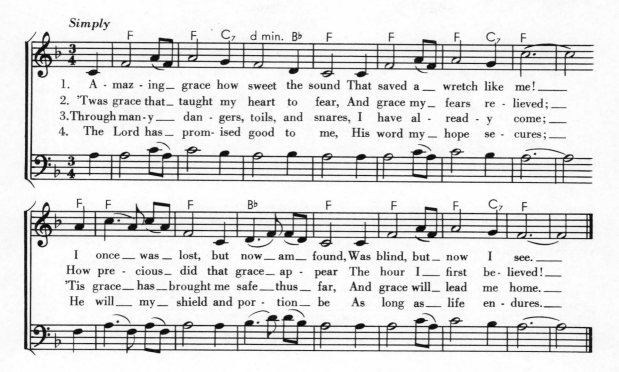

Simply

1. A - maz - ing_ grace how sweet the sound That saved a _ wretch like me! ____
2. 'Twas grace that_ taught my heart to fear, And grace my_ fears re - lieved; __
3. Through man - y __ dan - gers, toils, and snares, I have al - read - y come; __
4. The Lord has _ prom - ised good to me, His word my_ hope se - cures; __

I once _ was _ lost, but now _ am _ found, Was blind, but _ now I see. ____
How pre - cious_ did that grace_ ap - pear The hour I _ first be - lieved! __
'Tis grace_ has_ brought me safe_ thus_ far, And grace will_ lead me home. __
He will_ my_ shield and por - tion_ be As long as_ life en - dures. __

Praise and Thanksgiving

ALSATIAN ROUND

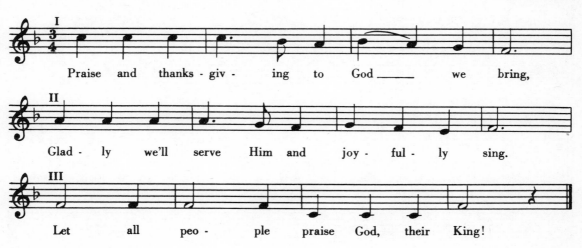

Praise and thanks - giv - ing to God _____ we bring,

Glad - ly we'll serve Him and joy - ful - ly sing.

Let all peo - ple praise God, their King!

O God, Beneath Thy Guiding Hand

MUSIC BY JOHN HATTON
WORDS BY LEONARD BACON

Jubilantly

1. O God! be-neath Thy guid-ing hand Our ex-iled fa-thers crossed the sea; And when they trod the win-try strand, With pray'r and psalm they wor-shipped Thee.

2. Law, free-dom, truth, and faith in God Came with those ex-iles o'er the waves; And where their pil-grim feet have trod, The God they trust-ed guards their graves.

3. And here Thy name, O God of love, Their chil-dren's chil-dren shall a-dore, Till these e-ter-nal hills re-move, And spring a-dorns the earth no more.

Holy God, We Praise Thy Name

TRADITIONAL MELODY
WORDS BY CLARENCE WALWORTH

1. Ho- ly God,___ we praise___ Thy name, Lord of all,___ we bow___ be- fore Thee; All on earth___ Thy scep- ter claim, All in heav'n___ a- bove___ a- dore Thee, In- fi- nite, Thy vast do- main, Ev- er- last- ing is___ Thy reign.

2. Hark! the loud___ ce- les- tial hymn, An- gel choirs___ a- bove___ are rais- ing! Cher- u- bim___ and Ser- a- phim In un- ceas- ing cho- rus prais- ing; Fill the heav'ns with sweet ac- cord, Ho- ly, ho- ly, ho- ly Lord.

Hark! The Vesper Hymn

MUSIC BY SIR JOHN ANDREW STEVENSON
WORDS BY THOMAS MOORE

1. Hark! the ves - per hymn is steal - ing O'er the wa - ters soft and clear;
2. Now like moon - light waves re - treat - ing To the shore, it dies a - long;

Near - er yet and near - er peal - ing, Soft it breaks up - on the ear.
Now, like an - gry surg - es meet - ing, Breaks the min - gled tide of song.

Ju - bi - la - te, Ju - bi - la - te, Ju - bi - la - te, A - men.

Far - ther now, now far - ther steal - ing, Soft it fades up - on the ear.
Hark! a - gain like waves re - treat - ing, To the shore it dies a - long.

Glory to Thee

MUSIC BY THOMAS TALLIS
WORDS BY THOMAS KEN

Glo - ry to Thee, my God, this night, For all the bless - ings of the light;

Keep me, oh, keep me, King of kings, Be - neath Thine own al - might - y wings.

O Come, O Come, Emmanuel

GREGORIAN HYMN
TRANSLATION BY JOHN MASON NEALE

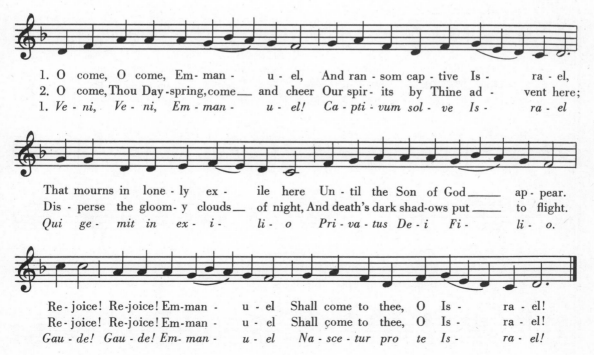

1. O come, O come, Em-man- u - el, And ran-som cap-tive Is- ra-el,
2. O come, Thou Day-spring, come and cheer Our spir-its by Thine ad- vent here;
1. *Ve - ni, Ve - ni, Em-man- u - el! Ca-pti-vum sol-ve Is- ra-el*

That mourns in lone-ly ex- ile here Un-til the Son of God ap-pear.
Dis-perse the gloom-y clouds of night, And death's dark shad-ows put to flight.
Qui ge-mit in ex- i- li - o Pri-va-tus De-i Fi- li- o.

Re-joice! Re-joice! Em-man- u - el Shall come to thee, O Is- ra-el!
Re-joice! Re-joice! Em-man- u - el Shall come to thee, O Is- ra-el!
Gau - de! Gau - de! Em-man- u - el Na-sce-tur pro te Is- ra-el!

In Dulci Jubilo

GERMAN CAROL

1. *In dul - ci ju - bi - lo!* _____ Let us our hom - age show! _____
2. *O pa - tris cha - ri - tas!* _____ *O na - ti le - ni - tas!*
3. *U - bi sunt gau - di - a,* _____ If that they be not there? _____

—— Our heart's joy re - clin - eth { *In prae - se - pi - o!* _____
—— Deep - ly were we stain - ed *Per nos - tra cri - mi - na.* _____
—— There are an - gels sing - ing { *No - va can - ti - ca;* _____

—— And like a bright star shin - eth *Ma - tris in gre - mi o!* _____
—— But Thou hast for us gain - ed *Coe - lo - rum gau - di - a.* _____
—— { There the bells are ring - ing, *In Re - gis cu - ri - a,* _____

—— *Al - pha es et O!* _____ *Al - pha es et O!*
O that we were there! _____ O that we were there!
O that we were there! _____ O that we were there!

Dona Nobis Pacem

TRADITIONAL ROUND

I.
Do - na no - bis pa - cem, pa - cem; do - na no - bis pa - cem.

II.
Do - na no - bis pa - cem; do - na no - bis pa - cem.

III.
Do - na no - bis pa - cem; do - na no - bis pa - cem.

I Am So Glad On Christmas Eve

NORWEGIAN CAROL
TRANSLATION BY P. A. SVEEGGEN

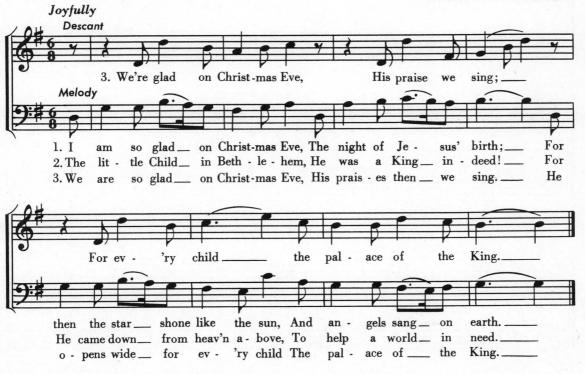

Joyfully

Descant

3. We're glad on Christ-mas Eve, His praise we sing;—

Melody

1. I am so glad— on Christ-mas Eve, The night of Je - sus' birth;— For
2. The lit - tle Child— in Beth - le - hem, He was a King— in - deed! For
3. We are so glad— on Christ-mas Eve, His prais - es then— we sing.— He

For ev - 'ry child ——— the pal - ace of the King.—

then the star— shone like the sun, And an - gels sang— on earth.——
He came down— from heav'n a - bove, To help a world— in need.——
o - pens wide— for ev - 'ry child The pal - ace of — the King.

Song of the Angels

MUSIC BY WILLIAM KNAPP
WORDS BY NAHUM TATE

While shep - herds watch'd their flocks by night, All seat - ed
on the ground, ____ An an - gel of the
Lord ___ came ___ down, And glo - ry, glo - - ry,
glo - - - ry shone ___ a - round. ____

While shep - herds watch'd their flocks, All seat - ed
on the ground, ____ An an - gel, an - gel of the
Lord ___ came ___ down, And ___ glo - ry, glo - - ry,
glo - - ry, glo - ry ___ shone a - round. ____

While Shepherds Watched Their Flocks by Night

MUSIC BY GEORGE FREDERIC HANDEL
WORDS BY NAHUM TATE

1. While __ shep-herds watched their flocks by __ night, All __ seat-ed on __ the __ ground, __ The __ an - gel of the Lord came __ down, And __ glo - ry shone a - round, __ And glo - ry shone a - round.

2. "Fear __ not," said he for might - y __ dread Had __ seized their trou - bled __ mind __ "Glad __ ti - dings of great joy I __ bring To __ you and all man - kind, __ To you and all man - kind.

3. "To __ you, in Da - vid's town this __ day, Is __ born of Da - vid's __ line __ The __ Sav - iour, who is Christ, the __ Lord, And __ this shall be the sign: __ And this shall be the sign:

4. "The __ heaven - ly Babe you there shall __ find To __ hu - man view dis - played, __ All __ mean - ly wrapped in swath - ing __ bands, And __ in a man - ger laid, __ And in a man - ger laid."

5. Thus spake the seraph, and forthwith
   Appeared a shining throng
   Of angels praising God, who thus
   Addressed their joyful song:

6. "All glory be to God on high,
   And to the earth be peace:
   Good will henceforth, from heaven to men,
   Begin and never cease!"

Who Can Retell?

JEWISH FOLK SONG
TRANSLATION BY B. M. EDIDIN

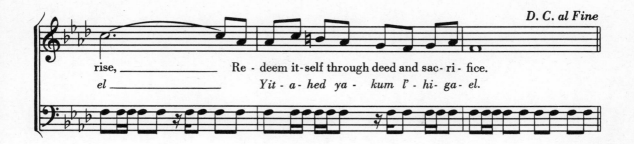

rise, _____ Re - deem it-self through deed and sac- ri - fice.
el _____ Yit - a - hed ya - kum l'- hi- ga- el.

Rocking

CZECH CAROL
TRANSLATION BY PERCY DEARMER

Gently

1. Lit - tle Je - sus, sweet-ly __ sleep, do not __ stir;
2. Mar - y's lit - tle ba - by, __ sleep, sweet-ly __ sleep;

We will __ lend you a coat of __ fur. We will rock you,
Sleep in __ com - fort, __ slum - ber __ deep. We will rock you,

rock you, rock you, Rock-ing to this lul - la - by. __ See the fur to
rock you, rock you, Rock you to this lul - la - by. __ We will serve you

keep you __ warm, Snug - ly __ round your __ ti - ny __ form.
all we __ can, Dar - ling, __ dar - ling __ lit - tle __ man.

83

Long, Long Ago

MUSIC BY JOHAN HYE-KNUDSEN
TRADITIONAL

Quietly

1. Winds through the ol - ive trees Soft - ly did blow,
2. Sheep on the hill - side lay Whit - er than snow,
3. Then from the hap - py sky An - gels bent low
4. For in a man - ger bed Cra - dled we know,

'Round lit - tle Beth - le - hem Long, long a - go.
Shep - herds were watch - ing them Long, long a - go.
Sing - ing their songs of joy Long, long a - go.
Christ came to Beth - le - hem Long, long a - go.

85

I Come from the Mountain

TRADITIONAL PUERTO RICAN CAROL
TRANSLATION BY MIRIAM L. TRANSUE

I come from the moun-tain to wor-ship a King, to bring Him a gift of a
Yo ba-jo del mon-te de ver un za-gal, trai-go un pa-ja-ri-llo que

bird that can sing. Then sing, lit-tle bird, at the won-der-ful sight, the
sa-be can-tar. Pues can-ta, bien mí-o, pues can-ta za-gal al

King who is born in a sta-ble to-night. Oh, won-der-ful sight,
Rey de los Cie-los que es-tá en un por-tal. Que es-tá en un por-tal,

Oh, won-der-ful sight, Lord of Light! Lord of Light!
que es-tá en un por-tal. ¡Es-cu-chad! ¡Es-cu-chad!

How sweet-ly sound His prais- es, how hap-py the mel-o-dies
¡Qué tri- nos tan dul- ces, qué a-le-gre y qué be-llo can-

ring ____ to wel-come His com-ing, the Heav-en-ly King, to
tar ____ Son las a-la-ban-zas al Rey Ce-les-tial, Son

wel-come His com-ing, the Heav-en-ly King. Heav'n-ly King. Heav'n-ly King!
las a-la-ban-zas al Rey Ce-les-tial, Ce-les-tial, Ce-les-tial!

From Ill Do Thou Defend Me

MELODY BY HANS LEO HASSLER
HARMONIZED BY J. S. BACH

From ill do Thou de- fend__ me; Re- ceive__ me, lead__ me home;
New bless-ings dai - ly send__ me; From Thee__ all good things come;

Thy__ love__ full__ oft __ in __ kind - ness hath milk and __ hon - ey __ giv'n;

O heal__ my__ mor- tal__ blind - ness, And fix__ my heart on Heav'n.

Bb Trumpets

Trombones

May the Good Lord Bless and Keep You

WORDS AND MUSIC BY MEREDITH WILLSON

May the Good Lord bless and keep you,— Wheth-er near or far a-way,

May you find that long a-wait-ed__ gold-en day to-day.
May the good you wish for oth-ers__ shine on you to-day.

May your trou-bles all be small ones,— And your for-tune ten times ten,
May your heart stay tuned to mu-sic,__ That will cheer the hearts of men,

May the Good Lord bless and keep you __ till we meet a-gain.

May you walk with sun-light shin-ing,__ And a blue-bird in ev-'ry tree,
long re-call the rain-bows,_ Then you'll soon for-get the rain,

May there be a sil-ver lin-ing__ Back of ev-'ry cloud you see.
May the warm and ten-der mem-'ries__ Be the ones that will re-main.

Fill your dreams with sweet to-mor-rows,— Nev-er mind what might have been,

May the Good Lord bless and keep you ___ till we meet ___ a - gain. May you

meet ___ a - gain; May the Good Lord bless and keep you till we

meet, ___ Till we meet ___ a - gain. ___
(Till we)

Silver and Gold

MUSIC BY MAX V. EXNER

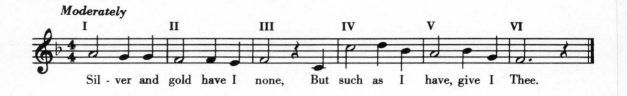

Sil - ver and gold have I none, But such as I have, give I Thee.

For the Beauty of the Earth

MUSIC BY CONRAD KOCHER
WORDS BY FOLLIOTT S. PIERPOINT

1. For the__ beau - ty of the earth, For the beau - ty of the skies,
2. For the__ won - der of each hour Of the day and of the night,
3. For the__ joy of ear and eye, For the heart and mind's de - light,
4. For the__ joy of hu - man love, Broth - er, sis - ter, par - ent, child,

For the__ love which from our birth O - ver and a - round us lies,
Hill and__ vale, and tree and flow'r, Sun and moon and stars of light,
For the__ mys - tic har - mo - ny Link - ing sense to sound and sight,
Friends on__ earth, and friends a - bove, For all gen - tle thoughts and mild,

Refrain

Lord of all, to Thee we raise This our hymn of grate - ful praise.

The American Hymn

WORDS AND MUSIC BY MATTHIAS KELLER

1. Speed our Re-pub-lic, O Fa-ther on high, Lead us in path-ways of jus-tice and right; Rul-ers as well as the ruled, one and all, Gir-dle with vir-tue, the ar-mor of might! Hail! three times hail — to our coun-try and flag! Rul-ers as well as the ruled, one and all,

2. Fore-most in bat-tle, for Free-dom to stand, We rush to arms when a-roused by its call; Still, as of yore when George Wash-ing-ton led, Thun-ders our war cry, "We con-quer or fall!" Hail! three times hail — to our coun-try and flag! Still, as of yore when George Wash-ing-ton led,

3. Rise up, proud ea-gle, rise up to the clouds, Spread thy broad wing o'er this fair west-ern world! Fling from thy beak our dear ban-ner of old! Show that it still is for free-dom un-furled! Hail! three times hail — to our coun-try and flag! Fling from thy beak our dear ban-ner of old!

Glory to Egypt

FROM "AÏDA"
MUSIC BY GIUSEPPE VERDI

Jubilantly

Glo - ry to E - gypt! Hail to thee! I - sis our strength and

Glo - ry to E - gypt! Hail to thee! I - sis our strength and

Glo - ry to E - gypt! Hail to thee! I - sis our strength and

pow'r! ___ The King of E - gypt tri - umphs! Sing hymns of praise and

pow'r! ___ The King of E - gypt tri - umphs! Sing hymns of praise and

pow'r! ___ The King of E - gypt tri - umphs! Sing hymns of praise and

ju - bi - la - tion on this glo - rious day! The lau - rel and the

ju - bi - la - tion this glo - rious day! The lau - rel and the

ju - bi - la - tion this glo - rious day! The lau - rel and the

lo - tus in their beau - ty on the vic - tor's brow, En -

lo - tus in their beau - ty on the brow, En -

lo - tus in their beau - ty on the brow, En -

twine in gar - lands sweet to veil the ar - mor, the spear, and the

twine in gar - lands sweet to veil ar - mor, the spear, and

twine in gar - lands sweet to veil ar - mor, the spear, and

94

The Letter

FROM "LA PÉRICHOLE"
MUSIC BY JACQUES OFFENBACH

Oh, to tell you of my real de-vo-tion I write you a let-ter to-day___ A-bout life and my deep-est e-mo-tion, for now I am go-ing a-

96

way.   You know that I   nev- er would leave you, And your heart— will tell you it's

true,___   In this sad   way we must now part,   dear,   It is best, and it's all we can

do.___   Oh,'tis hard to   be hap - py while hun - gry, I am sure that you know what I

mean,   And I sign"Per - i- chole"to   this let - ter As I long for the days that have

been!

Musetta's Waltz

FROM "LA BOHÈME"
MUSIC BY GIACOMO PUCCINI

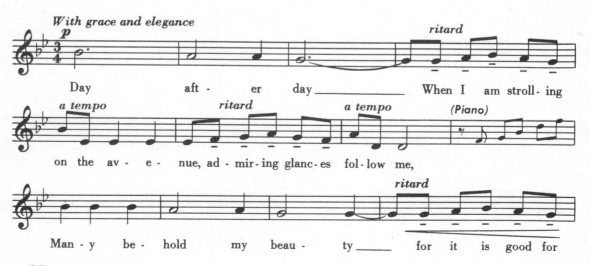

With grace and elegance

Day   aft - er   day _____   When I   am stroll - ing

on   the   av - e - nue,   ad - mir - ing glanc - es   fol - low   me,

Man - y   be - hold   my   beau - ty _____   for   it   is   good for

all to see, 'tis good for ev- 'ry- one to— see! And then I

love to see the fer- vent long- ing in the eyes of ev- 'ry - one who pass- es!

De - light fills my heart, — De - light fills my heart. —

Musetta

Day aft - er day ——— I know that you re -

Mimi

We plain- ly hear

mem - ber me, ——— How soon will you re- turn to me? ——— And

how Mu - set- ta feels when Mar- cel is near,

now you would for - get and say "good- by," ———

She loves him so, your friend Mar - cel; she is so much in

— but 'tis in vain, I know that we shall nev- er part, not you and— I!

love. ———

Even Bravest Heart May Swell

FROM "FAUST"
MUSIC BY CHARLES GOUNOD

E - ven brav-est heart may swell In the mo - ment of fare-well, Lov - ing smile of sis - ter kind, Qui - et home I leave be - hind. Oft shall I think of you when - e'er the wine-cup cir - cles round. When a - lone my watch I keep, And my com - rades lie a - sleep A - mong their arms up-on the tent - ed bat - tle ground.

100

The Star-Spangled Banner

MUSIC BY JOHN STAFFORD SMITH
WORDS BY FRANCIS SCOTT KEY

1. O___ say! can you see,___ by the dawn's ear - ly light, What so
2. On the shore dim - ly seen___ through the mists of the deep, Where the
3. O___ thus be it ev - er when___ free men shall stand Be -

proud - ly we hailed at the twi - light's last gleam - ing? Whose broad
foe's haugh - ty host in dread si - lence re - pos - es, What is
tween their loved homes and the war's des - o - la - tion! Blest with

stripes and bright stars, through the per - il - ous fight, O'er the
that which the breeze, o'er the tow - er - ing steep, As it
vic - t'ry and peace, may the heav'n - res - cued land Praise the

ram - parts we watched, were so gal - lant - ly stream - ing! And the
fit - ful - ly blows, half con - ceals, half dis - clos - es? Now it
Pow'r that hath made and pre - served us a na - tion, Then___

Through the clouds of the war the stars of
that banner still shone in my view, . . . Then,
in that hour of deliverance and joyful tri-
umph, my heart spoke; . . . "Does not such a
country and such defenders of their country
deserve a song?" . . . With it came an inspira-
tion not to be resisted; . . .

From a speech by Francis Scott Key at Frederick, Maryland.

rock - ets' red glare, the bombs burst - ing in air, Gave __
catch - es the gleam of the morn - ing's first beam, In full
con - quer we must, when our cause it is just, And __

proof through the night __ that our flag was still there.
glo - ry re - flect - ed now __ shines on the stream;
this be our mot - to: "In __ God is our trust!"

Refrain

O __ say, does that __ Star-Span - gled Ban - ner __ yet __ wave __ O'er the
'Tis the Star-Span-gled __ Ban - ner, O long may __ it __ wave __ O'er the
And the Star-Span-gled __ Ban - ner, in tri - umph __ shall __ wave __ O'er the

land __ of the free and the home of the brave?
land __ of the free and the home of the brave!
land __ of the free and the home of the brave!

THE UNITED STATES MARINE BAND is the oldest military band in the United States. It was organized at the same time as the Marine Corps itself by authorization of the Continental Congress in 1775. John Philip Sousa, conductor of the Band from 1880 to 1892, inaugurated the Band's annual nation-wide concert tour.

The United States Marine Band is officially considered "The President's Own" band. It plays at all White House functions and has played for every United States President except George Washington.

The Marines' Hymn

OFFICIAL SONG OF THE UNITED STATES MARINE CORPS

1. From the Halls of Mon-te-zu-ma To the shores of Trip-o-li; We fight our coun-try's bat-tles In the air, on land and sea; First to fight for

2. Our flag's un-furled to ev-'ry breeze From dawn to set-ting sun; We have fought in ev-'ry clime and place Where we could take a gun; In the snow of

3. Here's health to you and to our Corps Which we are proud to serve; In man-y a strife we've fought for life And nev-er lost our nerve; If the Ar-my

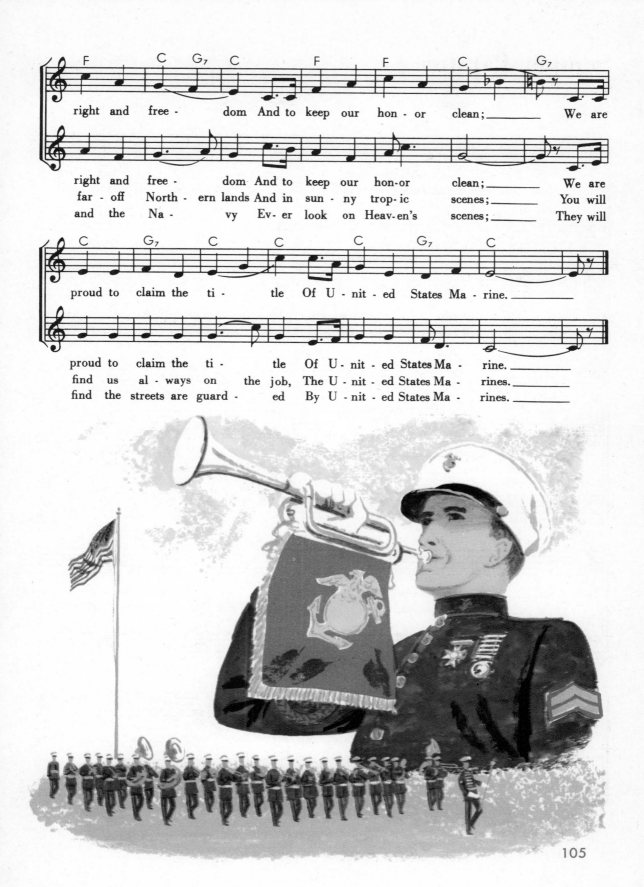

right and free - dom And to keep our hon - or clean;_____ We are

right and free - dom And to keep our hon - or clean;_____ We are
far - off North - ern lands And in sun - ny trop - ic scenes;_____ You will
and the Na - vy Ev - er look on Heav - en's scenes;_____ They will

proud to claim the ti - tle Of U - nit - ed States Ma - rine._____

proud to claim the ti - tle Of U - nit - ed States Ma - rine._____
find us al - ways on the job, The U - nit - ed States Ma - rines._____
find the streets are guard - ed By U - nit - ed States Ma - rines._____

Semper Paratus

WORDS AND MUSIC BY Capt. FRANCIS S. VAN BOSKERCK, U.S.C.G.

The Ramparts We Watch

MUSIC BY Lt. Com. W. GORDON BEECHER, U.S.N.
WORDS BY J. S. TOLDER II

Refrain

Stand forth for lib-er-ty un-til e-ter-ni-ty, God keep A-mer-i-ca, now, and ev-er-more! _____ For free-dom and for right al-ways we will fight. _____ And we nev-er will sur-ren-der _____ the ram-parts _____ we watch! _____

The Army Goes Rolling Along

H. W. ARBERG and Brig. Gen. EDMUND L. GRUBER, U. S. ARMY

Cadet Oath, United States Military Academy, West Point

"I, ... , do solemnly swear that I will support the Constitution of the United States, and bear true allegiance to the National Government; that I will maintain and defend the sovereignty of the United States, paramount to any and all allegiance, sovereignty, or fealty I may owe to any State, county, or country whatsoever; and that I will at all times obey the legal orders of my superior officers, and the rules and articles governing the armies of the United States."

From Shore to Shore

WORDS AND MUSIC BY NORMAN BELL

Jubilantly

mf

From shore to shore, in this great land we live in, there's a

new song in the air,_____ From shore to shore there's a

new birth of free - dom that will reach men ev - 'ry - where._____

We re - mem - ber the night when the dawn's ear - ly light found our

ban - ner still wav - ing for hon - or and right. So re - solve once a -

gain to keep free - dom's torch burn - ing for - ev - er and ev - er -

more_____ it will light the world from shore to shore._____

Gee, But I Want to Go Home

ARMY SONG
ADAPTED AND ARRANGED BY JOHN A. AND ALAN LOMAX

1. The cof-fee that they give us, They say is might-y fine, It's
2. The bis-cuits that they give us, They say are might-y fine,
3. The clothes that they give us, They say are might-y fine,

good for cuts and bruis-es And it tastes like i - o - dine.
One fell off a ta - ble And killed a pal of mine.
Me and my bud-dy Can both fit in - to mine.

Refrain

I don't want no more of ar - my life, Oh! Gee, but I

want to go, Gee, but I want to go home.

4. They treat us all like monkeys
   And make us stand in line,
   They give you fifty dollars a week
   And take back forty-nine.

5. The girls at the service club
   They say are mighty fine,
   Most are over eighty
   And the rest are under nine.

Alaska's Flag

MUSIC BY ELINOR DUSENBURY
WORDS BY MARIE DRAKE

Eight stars of gold on a field of blue, A - las - ka's flag;

May it mean to you the blue of the sea, the ev' - ning sky,

The moun - tain lakes and the flow'rs near - by; The gold of the ear - ly

sour - dough's dreams, The pre - cious gold of the hills and streams; The

bril - liant stars in the north - ern sky, The "Bear," the "Dip - per," and

shin - ing high, the great North star with its stead - y light, O'er

land and sea a bea - con bright, A - las - ka's flag to A -

las - kans dear, The sim - ple flag of a last fron - tier.

Our Fathers' God, to Thee, who art the author of our liberty, and under whom we have our freedom, we make our prayer. Make us ever mindful of the price that was paid to obtain that freedom and the cost that must be met to keep it. Help us in this Nation so to live it that other men shall desire it and seek after it. Believing in it, give us the backbone to stand up for it. Loving it, may we be willing to defend it.

Taken from a prayer offered by The Rev. Peter Marshall, D.D., Chaplain of the United States Senate 1947–1949, on Wednesday, April 9, 1947.

America

MUSIC BY HENRY CAREY
WORDS BY SAMUEL FRANCIS SMITH

With dignity

1. My coun - try! 'tis of thee, Sweet land of lib - er - ty,
2. My na - tive coun - try, thee, Land of the no - ble free,
3. Let mu - sic swell the breeze, And ring from all the trees
4. Our fa - thers' God, to Thee, Au - thor of lib - er - ty,

Of thee I sing; Land where my fa - thers died, Land of the
Thy name I love; I love thy rocks and rills, Thy woods and
Sweet Free - dom's song; Let mor - tal tongues a - wake, Let all that
To Thee we sing; Long may our land be bright With Free - dom's

Pil - grim's pride, From ev - 'ry moun - tain side Let free - dom ring.
tem - pled hills; My heart with rap - ture thrills Like that a - bove.
breathe par - take, Let rocks their si - lence break, The sound pro - long.
ho - ly light; Pro - tect us by Thy might, Great God, our King!

America, the Beautiful

MUSIC BY SAMUEL A. WARD
WORDS BY KATHERINE LEE BATES

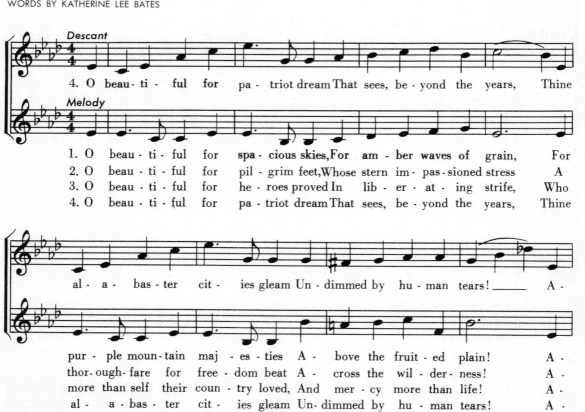

Descant

4. O beau - ti - ful for pa - triot dream That sees, be - yond the years, Thine

Melody

1. O beau - ti - ful for spa - cious skies, For am - ber waves of grain, For
2. O beau - ti - ful for pil - grim feet, Whose stern im - pas - sioned stress A
3. O beau - ti - ful for he - roes proved In lib - er - at - ing strife, Who
4. O beau - ti - ful for pa - triot dream That sees, be - yond the years, Thine

al - a - bas - ter cit - ies gleam Un - dimmed by hu - man tears! _____ A -

pur - ple moun - tain maj - es - ties A - bove the fruit - ed plain! A -
thor - ough - fare for free - dom beat A - cross the wil - der - ness! A -
more than self their coun - try loved, And mer - cy more than life! A -
al - a - bas - ter cit - ies gleam Un - dimmed by hu - man tears! A -

WHEN LILACS LAST IN THE DOORYARD BLOOM'D

Lo, body and soul – this land,

My own Manhattan with spires, and the sparkling and hurrying tides,
*   and the ships,*

The varied and ample land, the South and the North in the light,
*   Ohio's shores and flashing Missouri,*

And ever the far-spreading prairies cover'd with grass and corn.

Lo, the most excellent sun so calm and haughty,

The violet and purple morn with just-felt breezes,

The gentle soft-born measureless light,

The miracle spreading bathing all, the fulfill'd noon,

The coming eve delicious, the welcome night and the stars,

Over my cities shining all, enveloping man and land.

WALT WHITMAN

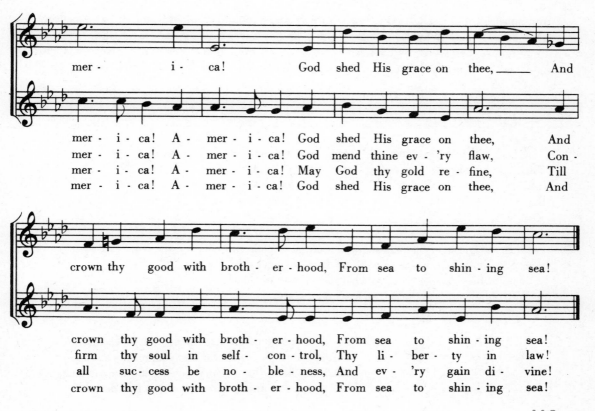

mer - i - ca! God shed His grace on thee,_____ And

mer - i - ca! A - mer - i - ca! God shed His grace on thee, And
mer - i - ca! A - mer - i - ca! God mend thine ev - 'ry flaw, Con -
mer - i - ca! A - mer - i - ca! May God thy gold re - fine, Till
mer - i - ca! A - mer - i - ca! God shed His grace on thee, And

crown thy good with broth - er - hood, From sea to shin - ing sea!

crown thy good with broth - er - hood, From sea to shin - ing sea!
firm thy soul in self - con - trol, Thy li - ber - ty in law!
all suc - cess be no - ble - ness, And ev - 'ry gain di - vine!
crown thy good with broth - er - hood, From sea to shin - ing sea!

The Day Columbus Landed

CANADIAN FOLK SONG (ADAPTED)

Gaily

1. 'Twas I who built the Rock-ies up and dug the five Great Lakes,
2. I nev-er shall for-get the day Co-lum-bus land-ed here.
3. I took him to the res-er-va-tion, there to meet the Chief,
4. Co-lum-bus was an hon-est man, but liked to make a "buck,"

And this I did with hoe and spade and just a few__ earth-quakes.
My-self and for-ty In-di-ans were right there on__ the pier.
Who greet-ed him po-lite-ly, though per-haps a tri-fle brief.
And blessed the hap-py chance that brought him such a slice__ of luck.

And then I built Ni-ag-ara Falls, rode o'er it on a deer,
He asked me, "Why do In-di-ans have feath-ers in their hair?"
Co-lum-bus asked, "What's cook-ing in the boil-er o-ver there?"
Said he, "I'll tel-e-vise this show and put it on the air,"

And__ that was man-y years be-fore Co-lum-bus land-ed here!
"Oh,__ that's to keep their trou-sers up," And this I do de-clare.
"That's a hep-cat in a hot__ spot," And this I do de-clare.
But he had to wait five hun-dred years, And this I do de-clare.

5. Now when the Queen of Spain heard what Columbus planned to do,
   She sent a wire, collect, which said, "Look here, my buckaroo,
   I've financed these shenanigins, so what makes with my share?"
   Our hero double-crossed the gal, and so I do declare.

6. So all you modern "guys and dolls" who have an urge to roam,
   Forget about the Seven Seas and plan to stay at home;
   You'll see the world in eighty days while sitting in a chair,
   By looking at your TV screen, and this I do declare.

My Grandma's Advice

OLD SONG

1. My — Grand-ma lives on yon-der lit-tle green, Fine old la-dy as
2. These — false young men they flat-ter and de-ceive, So, my love, you must
3. The first came a-court-ing was lit-tle John-ny Green, Fine young man as —

ev-er was seen; She — of-ten cau-tioned me — with — care Of
not — be-lieve; They'll — flatter, they'll coax, till you are in their snare, And a-
ev-er was seen; But the words of my Grand-ma run — in my head, And I

Refrain

all false young men — to be-ware. Tim-e-i tim-e um tum
way goes poor old — Grand-ma's care. Tim-e-i tim-e um tum
could not hear one — word he said. Tim-e-i tim-e um tum

tim-e um pa-ta, Of all false young men to be-ware.
tim-e um pa-ta, And a-way goes poor old Grand-ma's care.
tim-e um pa-ta, And I could not hear one word he said.

4. The next came a-courting was young Ellis Grove,
   'Twas then we met with a joyous love;
   With a joyous love I couldn't be afraid,
   You'd better get married than die an old maid.

5. Thinks I to myself there's some mistake,
   What a fuss these old folks make;
   If the boys and girls had all been so afraid,
   Then Grandma herself would have died an old maid!

117

I Know an Old Lady

MUSIC BY ALAN MILLS
WORDS BY ROSE BONNE

Lively—not fast

1. I know an old la-dy who swal-lowed a fly;
I don't know why she swal-lowed a fly! I guess she'll die!___ 2. I
know an old la-dy who swal-lowed a spi-der that wrig-gled and wrig-gled and
tick-led in-side her; She swal-lowed a spi-der to catch the fly, But
I don't know why she swal-lowed the fly. I guess she'll die!___

I know an old la-dy who swal-lowed a cat! Now, fan-cy that, to

bird! Now, how ab-surd, to
cat! Now, fan-cy that, to
dog! My, what a hog, to

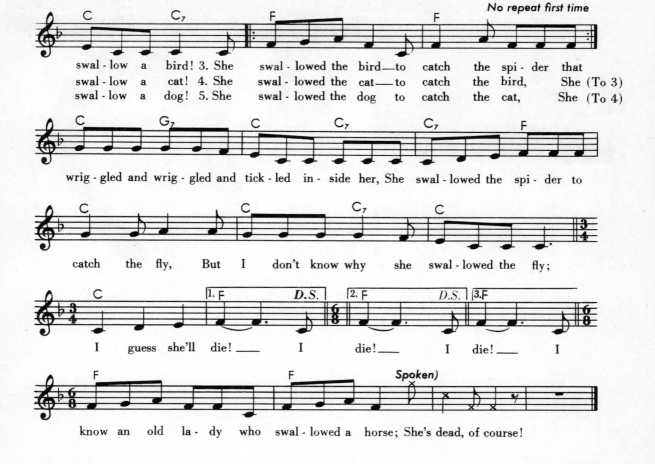

swal - low a bird! 3. She swal - lowed the bird—to catch the spi - der that
swal - low a cat! 4. She swal - lowed the cat—to catch the bird, She (To 3)
swal - low a dog! 5. She swal - lowed the dog to catch the cat, She (To 4)

wrig - gled and wrig - gled and tick - led in - side her, She swal - lowed the spi - der to

catch the fly, But I don't know why she swal - lowed the fly;

I guess she'll die! ___ I die! ___ I die! ___ I

know an old la - dy who swal - lowed a horse; She's dead, of course!

Dude Ranch Cowboy

WORDS AND MUSIC BY JIMMY EATON

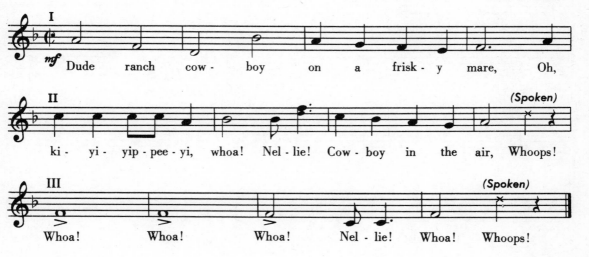

Dude ranch cow - boy on a frisk - y mare, Oh,

ki - yi - yip - pee - yi, whoa! Nel - lie! Cow - boy in the air, Whoops!

Whoa! Whoa! Whoa! Nel - lie! Whoa! Whoops!

I Found a Horseshoe

RAILROAD SONG FROM ILLINOIS AND IOWA

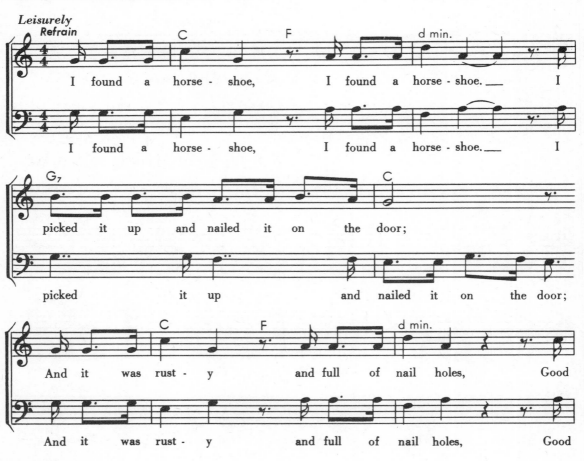

Leisurely
Refrain

I found a horse-shoe, I found a horse-shoe. I

I found a horse-shoe, I found a horse-shoe. I

picked it up and nailed it on the door;

picked it up and nailed it on the door;

And it was rust-y and full of nail holes, Good

And it was rust-y and full of nail holes, Good

120

luck 'twill bring to you for-ev - er - more. _____

luck 'twill bring to you for-ev - er - more. __

Verse

1. The man who owned the horse, he lived in New York, _____ The
2. The horse that wore the shoe, his name __ was Mike, _____ The

1. The man who owned the horse, he lived in New York, The
2. The horse that wore the shoe, his name __ was Mike, The

man who owned the horse, he lived in New York, _____ The
horse that wore the shoe, his name __ was Mike, _____ The

man who owned the horse, he lived in New York, The
horse that wore the shoe, his name __ was Mike, The

man who owned the horse, The man who owned the horse, The
horse that wore the shoe, The horse that wore the shoe, The

man who owned the horse, The man who owned the horse, The
horse that wore the shoe, The horse that wore the shoe, The

D. C. al Fine

man who owned the horse, he lived in New York. _____
horse that wore the shoe, his name __ was Mike. _____

man who owned the horse, he lived in New York, he lived in New York.
horse that wore the shoe, his name __ was Mike, his name __ was Mike.

That's Life

OLD ENGLISH

Merrily

1. Pray, lis - ten, I'll sing you a cute lit - tle song, It's not ver - y
2. My broth - er, a farm - er, once went to a fair, He pur - chased four

short, and it's not ver - y long; I'll tell you of things that have
hors - es, but one was a mare, An - oth - er is blind, and a

bright - ened my life, Since I fell in love and then took me a wife.
third can - not see, The fourth just es - caped from a glue fac - tor - y.

Refrain

Too - dle - ay, _____ too - dle - ay, _____

Too - dle - ay, too - dle - ay,

Oh, I've nev - er kept chick - ens be - fore in my life.

3. One day I went out to see my Uncle Jim,
   He said someone had been throwing tomatoes at him;
   "Tomatoes don't hurt, sir," said I, with a grin,
   He said, "Oh, yes they do, when they're packed in a tin."

4. The next day I went to see Johnny McBrown,
   He was having a bath, and he couldn't come down;
   I said, "Slip on something, and come down if you can,"
   So he slipped on the soap and came down with a bang!

122

The Sow Took the Measles

AMERICAN FRONTIER SONG

Refrain

How do you think I be-gan in the world? I got me a sow and

sev-'ral oth-er thing. The sow took the mea-sles and she died in the spring.

Verse

1. What do you think I made of her hide? The ver-y best sad-dle that you
2. What do you think I made of her nose? The ver-y best thim-ble that
3. What do you think I made of her tail? The ver-y best whup that
4. What do you think I made of her feet? The ver-y best pick-les that you

ev-er did ride.___ Sad-dle or bri-dle or an-y such thing,___
ev-er sewed clothes.___ Thim-ble or thread___ or an-y such thing,___
ev-er sought sail.___ Whup or whup-sock-et, or an-y such thing,___
ev-er did eat.___ Pick-les or glue___ or an-y such thing,___

The

sow took the mea-sles and she died in the spring.

123

Multiplication Is Vexation

MID-19TH CENTURY ENGLISH

Mul - ti - pli - ca - tion is vex - a - tion, Di - vi - sion is as bad; The

rule of these it puz - zles me, And prac - tice makes me mad.

John Grumlie

SCOTTISH FOLK SONG

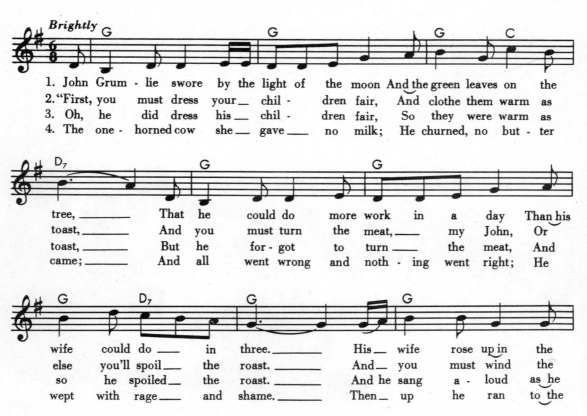

Brightly

1. John Grum - lie swore by the light of the moon And the green leaves on the
2. "First, you must dress your _ chil - dren fair, And clothe them warm as
3. Oh, he did dress his _ chil - dren fair, So they were warm as
4. The one - horned cow she _ gave _ no milk; He churned, no but - ter

tree, _____ That he could do more work in a day Than his
toast, _____ And you must turn the meat, _ my John, Or
toast, _____ But he for - got to turn _ the meat, And
came; _____ And all went wrong and noth - ing went right; He

wife could do _ in three. _____ His _ wife rose up in the
else you'll spoil _ the roast. _____ And _ you must wind the
so he spoiled _ the roast. _____ And he sang a - loud as he
wept with rage _ and shame. _____ Then up he ran to the

124

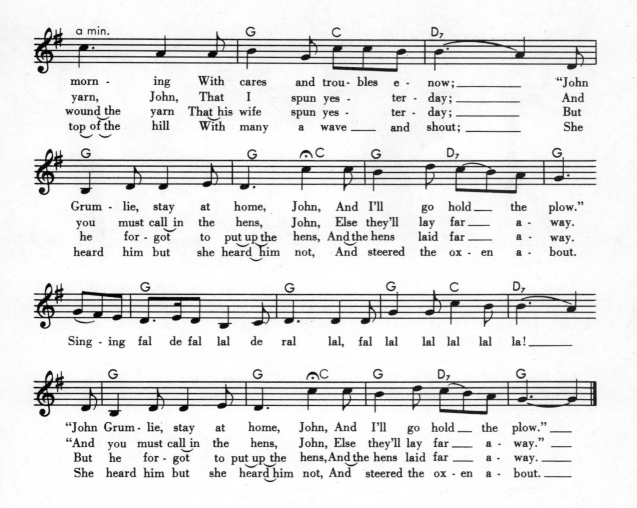

morn - ing With cares and trou - bles e - now; _____ "John
yarn, John, That I spun yes - ter - day; _____ And
wound the yarn That his wife spun yes - ter - day; _____ But
top of the hill With many a wave _____ and shout; _____ She

Grum - lie, stay at home, John, And I'll go hold _____ the plow."
you must call in the hens, John, Else they'll lay far _____ a - way.
he for - got to put up the hens, And the hens laid far _____ a - way.
heard him but she heard him not, And steered the ox - en a - bout.

Sing - ing fal de fal lal de ral lal, fal lal lal lal lal la! _____

"John Grum - lie, stay at home, John, And I'll go hold _____ the plow." _____
"And you must call in the hens, John, Else they'll lay far _____ a - way." _____
But he for - got to put up the hens, And the hens laid far _____ a - way. _____
She heard him but she heard him not, And steered the ox - en a - bout. _____

5. John Grumlie's wife came home at eve,
   But laughed, as she'd been mad
   When she saw the house in such a plight,
   And John so glum and sad.
   Said he, "I give up my job at home,
   I'll be no more a wife."
   "Indeed," said she, "I'm well content,
   You may keep it the rest of your life."

6. " 'Tis no fair exchange," said surly John.
   "I'll do as I've done before."
   With that his good wife pretended to roar,
   And John made off to the door.
   "Stop, stop, sweet wife, I'll say no more,
   You know I'll never roam;
   But henceforth I will mind the plow,
   And you will stay at home."

The Deaf Woman's Courtship

AMERICAN FOLK SONG

Boys

f 1. "Old wom-an, old wom-an, will you go a-shear - ing?"
mf 2. "Old wom-an, old wom-an, will you go a-walk - ing?"
p 3. "Old wom-an, old wom-an, will you do my knit - ting?"

Girls

p "Speak a lit-tle loud-er, Sir, I'm rath-er thick of hear - ing."
mf "Speak a lit-tle loud-er, Sir, I scarce-ly hear you talk - ing."
f "Hear-ing's get-ting bet-ter now, come near-er where I'm sit - ting."

Boys   **Girls**

f "Old wom-an, old wom-an, are you fond of spin - ning?" *p* "Just___
mf "Old wom-an, old wom-an, are you good at weav - ing?" *mf* "Pray,
pp "Old wom-an, old wom-an, will you come and kiss___ me?" *f* "I___

speak a lit-tle loud-er, Sir, I on-ly see you grin - ning."
speak a wee bit loud-er, Sir, my hear-ing is de-ceiv - ing."
thank you ver-y kind-ly, Sir, I hear you now quite clear-ly."

126

Bones

AMERICAN FOLK SONG

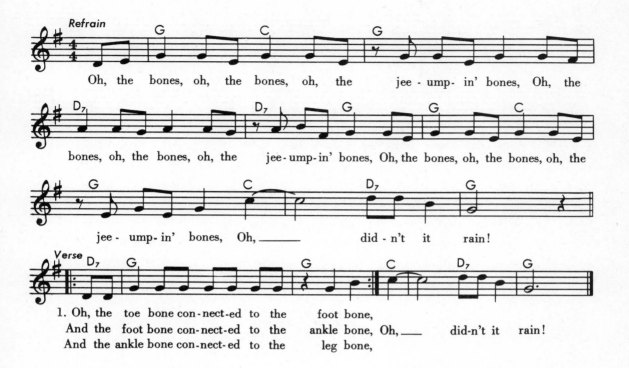

Refrain

Oh, the bones, oh, the bones, oh, the jee-ump-in' bones, Oh, the

bones, oh, the bones, oh, the jee-ump-in' bones, Oh, the bones, oh, the bones, oh, the

jee-ump-in' bones, Oh,_____ did-n't it rain!

Verse

1. Oh, the toe bone con-nect-ed to the foot bone,
And the foot bone con-nect-ed to the ankle bone, Oh,___ did-n't it rain!
And the ankle bone con-nect-ed to the leg bone,

2. Oh, the leg bone connected to the knee bone,
And the knee bone connected to the thigh bone,
And the thigh bone connected to the hip bone,

3. Oh, the hip bone connected to the back bone,
And the back bone connected to the neck bone,
And the neck bone connected to the head bone.

4. Oh, the finger bone connected to the hand bone,
And the hand bone connected to the elbow bone,
And the elbow bone connected to the shoulder bone,

5. Oh, the shoulder bone connected to the back bone,
And the back bone connected to the neck bone,
And the neck bone connected to the head bone.

127

Vas Is Dis?

PENNSYLVANIA FOLK SONG

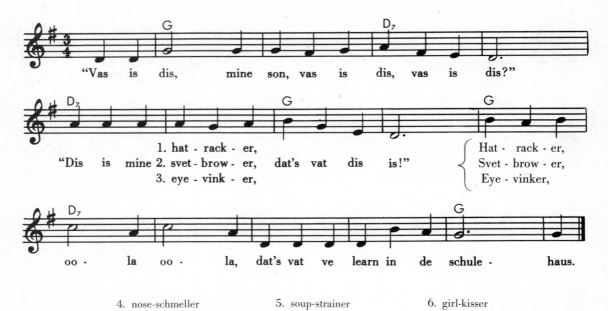

"Vas is dis, mine son, vas is dis, vas is dis?"

"Dis is mine
1. hat - rack - er,
2. svet - brow - er, dat's vat dis is!"
3. eye - vink - er,

{ Hat - rack - er,
Svet - brow - er,
Eye - vinker,

oo - la oo - la, dat's vat ve learn in de schule - haus.

4. nose-schmeller   5. soup-strainer   6. girl-kisser

Beautiful

AMERICAN FOLK SONG
COLLECTED AND ADAPTED BY JOHN A. AND ALAN LOMAX

1. Ain't it fierce to be so beau - ti - ful, beau - ti - ful, So rar - in', tear in'
2. Ain't it fierce to be so brain - y, brain - y, So rar' - in', tear in'

beau - ti - ful, beau - ti - ful! I ain't got no peace of mind, _____
brain - y, brain - y! I ain't got no peace of mind, The

Ev - 'ry - bod - y is so aw - ful - ly kind. Out - side of my door they
profs _____ they _____ are so aw - ful - ly kind. Out - side of their doors they

stand,___ stand,___ Wait - in' for my heart and hand,___ hand,___
stand,___ stand,___ Wait - in' for to shake my hand,___ hand,___

(Spoken)

Al - most ev - 'ry sin - gle hour, Some - one's sure to
Al - most ev - 'ry sin - gle day, Some - one's sure to

send me flowers. Ain't it fierce to be so beau - ti - ful!
give me "A." Ain't it fierce to be so brain - y!

Everybody Loves Saturday Night

GHANA FOLK SONG

Ev - 'ry - bod - y loves Sat - ur - day night,

Ev - 'ry - bod - y loves Sat - ur - day night.

Ev - ry - bod - y, Ev - ry - bod - y, Ev - 'ry - bod - y, Ev - 'ry - bod - y,

Ev - 'ry - bod - y loves Sat - ur - day night.

Piano (Repeat as needed)

Dixie

WORDS AND MUSIC BY DAN EMMETT

I _ wish I was _ in the land of cot - ton, Old times there are
Dix - ie land _ where _ I was born _ Ear - ly on a

not for - got - ten, Look a - way, A - way, A - way, Dix - ie
frost - y morn - in', Look a - way, look a - way, Dix - ie

1. land. In _ land. I wish I was in Dix - ie, Hoo - ray! Hoo - ray! Hoo -
2.

ray! Hoo - ray! In Dix - ie land I'll take my stand To live and die in

A - way A - way,
Dix - ie, A - way, A - way, a - way down South in

A - way A - way
Dix - ie. A - way, A - way, a - way down South, in Dix - ie!

Deep in the Heart of Texas

MUSIC BY DON SWANDER
WORDS BY JUNE HERSHEY

131

Let It Snow! Let It Snow! Let It Snow!

MUSIC BY JULE STYNE
WORDS BY SAMMY CAHN

The snow-man in the yard is froz-en hard; He's a sor-ry sight to see,

If he had a brain, he'd com-plain, Bet he wish-es he were me.

Refrain

Oh, the weath-er out-side is fright-ful, Ooo _____

Ooo _____ But the fire is so de-

And since we've no place to go, Let it snow! Let it snow! Let it

light-ful, Ooo _____ Doo doo doo doo

snow! It does-n't show signs of stop-ping, Ooo _____

Ooo _____ And I brought some corn for

The lights are turn'd 'way down low, Let it snow! Let it snow! Let it

pop-ping; Ooo _____ Doo doo doo doo

132

snow! When we fi-nal-ly kiss good-night,

How I'll hate go-ing out in the

But if you'll real-ly hold me tight, Ooo _____

storm! But if you'll real-ly hold me tight, All the way home I'll be

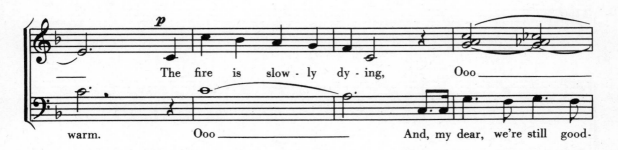

The fire is slow-ly dy-ing, Ooo _____

warm. Ooo _____ And, my dear, we're still good-

But as long as you love me so, Let it snow! Let it

bye-ing, Ooo _____ Doo doo doo doo Let it snow!

snow! Let it snow! Let it snow! Let it snow!

Let it snow! Let it snow! Let it snow! Let it snow! Let it snow!

Jingle Bells

WORDS AND MUSIC BY J. PIERPONT

Dash- ing through the snow in a one - horse o - pen sleigh,

Dash - - ing through the snow in o - pen

O'er the fields we go, laugh- ing all the way;

sleigh. O'er fields we go a - laugh- ing all the

Bells on Bob - tail ring, mak- ing spir - its bright. What

way; The bells are ring - - ing clear and

fun it is to laugh and sing a sleigh - ing song to - night!

bright. What fun to ride to - night!

El Capitan

FROM "EL CAPITAN"
WORDS AND MUSIC BY JOHN PHILIP SOUSA

(Whistle)

You see in me, my friends, a man of con-sum-mate brav-er-y; My in-most na-ture tends to free the world from all slav-er-y, This thought then cher-ish: Though you per-ish, Crush out Span-ish knav-er-y. ___ Be-hold El Cap-i-tan; ___ Gaze on his mis-an-throp-ic stare, No-tice his pen-e-trat-ing glare; Come match him if you can. ___ He is the cham-pi-on be-yond com-pare. ___

(Piano)

A-gainst the Span-ish ar-my I must

My Name Is John Wellington Wells

FROM "THE SORCERER"
MUSIC BY ARTHUR SULLIVAN
WORDS BY W. S. GILBERT

My name is John Well-ing-ton Wells,_____ I'm a

deal-er in mag-ic and spells,_____ In bless-ings and curs-es And

ev-er-fill'd purs-es, In proph-e-cies, witch-es, and

knells._____ If you want a proud foe to "make tracks"_____ If you'd

melt a rich un-cle in wax_____ You've but to look in on the

res-i-dent Djinn, Num-ber sev-en-ty, Sim-mer-y

Axe. We've a first-rate as-sort-ment of mag-ic; And for

rais-ing a post-hu-mous shade, With ef-fects that are com-ic or

trag - ic, There's no cheap- er house in the trade._____ Love-

phil - tre, we've quan - ti - ties of it! And for

crescendo

knowl-edge if an - y - one burns,_____ We're keep- ing a ver - y small

f   *p*

proph- et, a proph- et who brings us un - bound-ed re - turns_____ My

name is John Well - ing - ton Wells,_____ I'm a

deal - er in mag - ic and spells,_____ In bless-ings and curs - es, and

ev - er - fill'd purs - es, In proph - e - cies, witch - es, and

knells._____ And if an - y - one an - y - thing lacks,_____ He'll

p

find it all read - y in stacks,_____ If he'll on - ly look in on the

res - i - dent Djinn, Num- ber sev- en - ty, Sim- mer - y Axe!_____

f

Give Me Your Tired, Your Poor

MUSIC BY IRVING BERLIN
WORDS FROM THE POEM "THE NEW COLOSSUS" BY EMMA LAZARUS

140

shore. _____ Send these, the home-less, tem-pest-tossed to

shore. _____ Send these, the tem- pest- tossed to _____

shore. _____ Send these, the tem- pest- tossed to

me, I lift my lamp be-side the gold- en door!"

me. _____ I lift my lamp be-side the gold- en door!"

me, I lift my lamp be-side the gold- en door!"

(continued →)

A cappella

p

Hmmm _____ Hmmm _____

"Give me your tired, your poor, _____ Your hud-dled mass-es

Hmmm _____ Hmmm _____

yearn-ing to breathe free, _____ The wretch-ed ref-use of your teem-ing

Hmmm _____

f

Hmmm _____ Hmmm ____

shore, _____ Send these, the home-less, tem-pest-tossed to

____ Hmmm _____ Hmmm _____

Hmmm _____

me, I lift my lamp be-side the gold-en door!"

____ Hmmm _____ Hmmm _____

142

I See the Moon

WORDS AND MUSIC BY MEREDITH WILLSON

1. I see the moon, the moon sees me, Down through the leaves of the old oak tree, Please let the light that shines on me Shine on the one I love.

2. I hear the lark, the lark hears me, Sing-ing a song with a mem-o-ry, Please let the lark that sings to me Sing to the one I love.

O-ver the moun-tain, O-ver the sea, Back where my heart is long-ing to be,

Please let the light that shines on me Shine on the one I love.
Please let the lark that sings to me Sing to the one I love.

While Strolling Through the Park

WORDS AND MUSIC BY ED HALEY

While strolling through the park one day, In the mer-ry, mer-ry month of May, I was tak-en by sur-prise by a pair of ro-guish eyes, In a mo-ment my poor heart was stole a-way. A

144

Romany Life

FROM "THE FORTUNE TELLER"
MUSIC BY VICTOR HERBERT
WORDS BY HARRY B. SMITH

Through the for-est, wild and free, Sounds our Mag-yar

mel - o - dy; Ev - er danc-ing, none can be Half so

mer - ry __ as are __ we. Through the for-est, wild and free,

Sounds the Mag-yar mel - o - dy; Ev - er danc-ing,

as they say, None so mer - ry, __ and none so gay. __

Fast - er twirl - ing! Ju - che! with leap and bound, Ho! Dance, __ Ay, dance, Zi-

geu - ner, to mu-sic's sound; Sing - ing ev - er! Ju - che! Our

song is gay, Ho! sing, __ Ay, sing, Zi- geu - ner while yet ye may.

Through the for-est, wild and free, Sounds our Mag-yar

In the Good Old Summer Time

MUSIC BY GEORGE EVANS
WORDS BY REN SHIELDS

In the good old sum-mer time, _____ In the good old

In the good old sum-mer time, _____ In the good old

Sum-mer time, good old

The Happy Wanderer

MUSIC BY FRIEDRICH W. MOLLER
WORDS BY ANTONIA RIDGE

With a steady beat

1. I love to go a wan-der-ing, A-long the
2. I love to wan-der by the stream That danc-es
3. I wave my hat to all I meet, And they wave

moun-tain track, _____ And as I go, I
in the sun, _____ So joy-ous-ly it
back to me, _____ And black birds call so

love to sing, My knap-sack on my back. _____
calls to me, "Come! Join my hap-py song!" _____
loud and sweet From ev-'ry green-wood tree. _____

Whistle 2nd time

Val - de ri, Val - de ra, _____ Val - de
Val - de ri, Val - de ra,

ra, _____ Val - de ha, ha, ha, ha, ha, ha, Val - de ri, _____
Val - de ra, Val - de ha, ha, ha, ha, ha, ha, Val - de

Val- de- ra, _____ My knap - sack on my back. _____
"Come! Join my hap - py song!" _____
From ev - 'ry green - wood tree. _____

ri, Val- de ra,

4. High over head, the skylarks wing,
   They never rest at home,
   But just like me, they love to sing,
   As o'er the world we roam.

5. Oh, may I go a-wandering
   Until the day I die!
   Oh, may I always laugh and sing,
   Beneath God's clear blue sky!

Tell Me Why

TRADITIONAL

Tenderly

1. Tell __ me why __ the stars do shine, Tell __ me why __ the
2. God __ has made __ the stars to shine, God __ has made __ the

i - vy twines, Tell __ me why __ the skies are blue,
i - vy twine, God __ has made __ the skies so blue,

And I will tell you why I _____ love you.
And God has made you, that's why I love you.

ritenuto

incalzando

ritenuto

incalzando

153

The music notation on pages 152 and 153 is an excerpt from the *full score* of a famous symphony.

A full score is a clear and complete picture of what the composer had in mind when he wrote the music. It shows the part assigned to every instrument, measure by measure. That is why a conductor reads from a full score. At all times during the performance, he knows what instruments should be playing and how they should sound.

As you study the full score on the preceding pages, you will discover why a conductor uses a special language of gestures as he guides his orchestra in interpreting the ideas of the composer. You will see how a composer translates musical ideas into music notation. In a way, you will sense what it is like to play in an orchestra.

Notice that the melody and a brief counter-melody are colored in red. The names of the instruments and words which tell how the instruments should be played are colored in yellow. Marks and words on the score, colored in blue, guide the conductor and the instrumentalists in creating the kind of sound the composer intended. The notation of the accompaniment appears in black.

Do you recognize the melody played by the violins? This melody, the brief counter-melody, and the chords used in the accompaniment have been extracted from the full score and arranged so that you can sing this part of *Symphony No. 6* by Tchaikovsky.

Excerpts from other musical compositions appear on pages 154–161. They include melodies that are known and enjoyed by people all over the world.

Peter Ilich Tchaikovsky (1840–1893)

Symphony No. 6: Movement 1, Measures 130–138

Felix Mendelssohn (1809–1847)

A Midsummer Night's Dream: Nocturne, Measures 1–16

César Franck (1822–1890)

Sonata for Piano and Violin: Movement 4, Measures 1–8

Alexander Borodin (1833–1887)

String Quartet No. 2: Scherzo, Measures 29–36

String Quartet No. 2 (continued): Nocturne, Measures 1–8

N. A. Rimsky-Korsakoff (1844–1908)

Scheherazade: Movement 3, The Young Prince and the Princess, Measures 1–18

Franz Schubert (1797–1828)

Symphony No. 8: Movement 1, Measures 1–20

Symphony No. 8 (continued): Movement 1, Measures 44–52

Johannes Brahms (1833–1897)

Symphony No. 2: Movement 1, Measures 2–9

Symphony No. 2 (continued): Movement 1, Measures 82–89

Zoltán Kodály (1882—)

Háry-János: Suite, Viennese Musical Clock, Measures 5–12

160

Igor Stravinsky (1882—)

The Firebird: Dance of the Princesses, Measures 17–32

Sounds in Rhythm

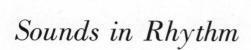

THE INSTRUMENTS in the illustration are used in performing all kinds of music. You may have seen some of them in your school band or orchestra. They are seen frequently on television programs. Can you name each instrument?

Play the instruments one at a time. Which ones do you play by striking? by beating? by shaking? by rubbing? Which instrument is played by striking *and* shaking? Make sure that you use the correct playing technique. Describe the sound of each instrument in words. Listen carefully. At first, some of them may sound very much alike. Can you control the sound? Make it loud and then soft. Can you make it fast? slow? short? long?

Some of these instruments are made in different sizes. This affects the pitch of the sound. For example, a small drum sounds "high." A big drum sounds "low." But remember, a drum of any size still has the distinctive sound of a drum.

The sounds produced by the instruments in the illustration can be combined in many ways. The arrangements in "Sounds in Rhythm" are just a starting point. You can create your own arrangements using the instruments in the illustration and others of the same type. As you work out the arrangements which follow, pay careful attention to tempo and dynamic markings—and play with skill.

162

ARRANGEMENT I

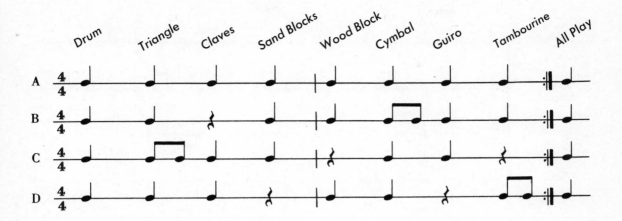

ARRANGEMENT II

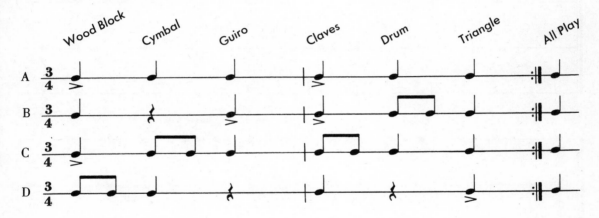

ARRANGEMENT III

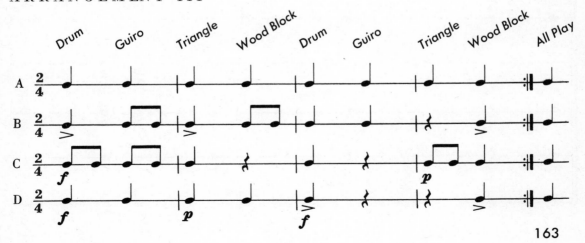

ARRANGEMENT IV

ARRANGEMENT V

Records by the Billion

Mr. Edison's Wonderful "Talking Machine"

ONE DAY in the year 1877, the famous inventor Thomas A. Edison was working in his laboratory at Menlo Park, New Jersey. Before him, on his table, was a strange-looking machine. It had been built by one of Edison's assistants from plans drawn up by the inventor. No one had ever seen anything like it before.

box, from one side of which extended a horn shaped something like a small megaphone. Attached to the other side of the box was a needle which just touched the surface of the tin foil.

Slowly, Edison began to turn the crank. As he did so the cylinder revolved, the round box moved slowly along its slide, and the

A model of one of Edison's first talking machines

A famous experiment

As you can see in the picture, Edison's machine consisted of a long cylinder, mounted on an axle. At one end of the axle was a crank. At the other end was a small flywheel. The cylinder was covered by a sheet of thin tin foil. Mounted on a slide, close to the surface of the cylinder, was a flat, round

needle began pressing a spiral groove into the surface of the foil. Bringing his mouth close to the open end of the horn, Edison spoke, slowly and clearly.

"Mary had a little lamb," he said, and continued the words of the famous nursery rhyme.

Then, after moving the needle back to its

starting point, Edison again began to turn the crank. At first only a few faint sounds came from the horn. But then, suddenly, there was a voice in the horn—rough and scratchy, but still a voice—Edison's voice.

"Mary had a little lamb," it said. Edison's wonderful "talking machine" was born.

From air waves to record grooves

It is not hard to understand how Edison's machine worked, if you remember that sound travels through the air in the form of waves. These air waves are much like the waves that spread out on the surface of a pond when you toss a stone into the water. When a drummer strikes the head of his drum the tightly-stretched skin vibrates rapidly. As it does so, it pushes the air back and forth and starts a series of waves which spread out rapidly in all directions. When these air waves reach your ear, they cause the tiny "drum head" inside your ear to vibrate at the same rate as the big drum. This sends a message to your brain—you "hear" the drum beat.

In Edison's talking machine, a thin round piece of metal called a *diaphragm* was substituted for the eardrum. The small horn picked up the air waves set up by Edison's voice and "focused" them on the diaphragm much as a camera lens focuses light on the film. As the diaphragm vibrated, the needle attached to it moved rapidly up and down and pressed "waves" into the surface of the moving tin foil. Then, when the needle was moved back to the starting point and the cylinder again began to turn, the wavy groove caused the needle and diaphragm to vibrate just as they had before. The diaphragm, like a tiny drum head, set up a new series of air waves, and Edison's words came back to him. The drawing at the right will help you to see how this worked.

It was really a simple idea that Edison had. But no one had ever thought of it before. Most great inventions are the result of several men's work. When an inventor sends a model or drawing of his invention to the Patent Office in Washington, he usually finds that others have had ideas very much like his own. Often he cannot have his idea patented because someone else thought of it first. But when Edison applied for a patent on his "phonograph," as he called it, there was no record of any such machine in the Patent Office.

A great invention—but still only a toy

On that day in 1877 Edison demonstrated the basic principle of the phonograph. The energy of sound waves in the air can be used to cut grooves in the surface of a record. These grooves "store up" the sound that caused them and can be used to re-create that sound at a later time. This same principle is

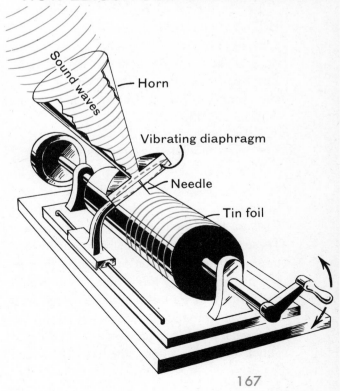

HOW EDISON'S MACHINE WORKED

Sound waves

Horn

Vibrating diaphragm

Needle

Tin foil

167

the basis of every modern phonograph and record player.

Edison's little talking machine demonstrated the idea. But it was not good for much else. The quality of the sound that came from the horn was poor indeed. The tin foil cylinder could only be played once or twice before it wore out and it could not even be removed from the machine. Nor was there any way to make copies of the cylinder. Finally, the machine had to be cranked by hand. It was very difficult to turn the cylinder at an even speed. As a result, musical sounds would not stay on pitch.

Three basic improvements were necessary before the phonograph could become a useable instrument for home entertainment. First, a material better than tin foil had to be found for making records. This material would have to take smooth, clean-cut grooves and be durable enough so that the record could be played over and over again. Second, some method would have to be developed for making exact copies of the original record in large quantities. Finally, a motor would have to be built that would run the machine at a constant, even speed. It was many years before all of these improvements were successfully worked out, but Edison had demonstrated the basic idea.

How Edison's Idea Was Developed by Others

Having proved that his idea would work, Edison put aside his crude phonograph and did no further work on it for several years. He knew that it could be improved, but at the time he was more interested in developing other ideas—among them the electric light. But other men took up where Edison left off and went to work to improve the original "talking machine."

First on the market—the Graphophone

First to become interested in Edison's invention were two men, Charles Tainter and Chichester Bell—a relative of Alexander Graham Bell, the inventor of the telephone. These two men tackled the first of the needed improvements to Edison's machine—the record material. They knew that people would not want to buy a talking machine unless it used *interchangeable* records—that is, the user must be able to take off one record and put on another as often as he liked. They also knew that the records must be durable enough to last through many playings.

After years of experimenting, Tainter and Bell developed a cylinder made of paper coated with a layer of hard wax. They also made improvements in the method of cutting the grooves on the cylinder which gave more natural sound. With these improvements, Tainter and Bell thought that they had a machine which could be sold, and in 1887 they put it on the market. They called it the *Graphophone*.

Almost from the start the Graphophone was a success. People bought it, and began to collect cylinders to play on it. The music, chiefly vocal numbers, that was recorded on these cylinders came out sounding tinny and scratchy. The machine still had to be cranked by hand. But it did work, and the records could be played over and over to open-mouthed audiences. It was one of the wonders of the age.

Meanwhile, Edison had dusted off his original talking machine, improved it, and put it on the market as the Edison Phonograph. Visitors to the Chicago World's Fair in 1893 thronged to see an attraction called the "Edison Automatic Phonograph Parlour." Here, after paying a coin, one could pick up a long tube with an earpiece on one end and listen to a popular song. The machine was so popular that it soon wore out, but here was the original "juke box."

The hard-working singers

As the Edison Phonograph and the Graphophone became more popular, the demand for records grew rapidly. This made a problem for the record-makers, for there was still no way of making exact copies in quantity of an original recording. Each record was one-of-a-kind.

the horns as loudly as he could. The louder he sang, the better the record—whether the music was supposed to be loud or not. The recording machines closest to the artist produced the best records.

In this way 20 recordings of a song could be made at once. But this was not nearly enough. The perspiring artist often had to sing the same song as many as 60 times in one day. Really fine artists, of course, were not interested in going through this ordeal for the low pay they would receive. But it made little difference. A poor voice sounded much the same as a beautiful one on those early records.

The disk record solves the problem

For a time there seemed to be little hope for the hard-working singers. In spite of much effort and many experiments, no one

An early recording session

A recording session, in the early days of the phonograph, was a strange sight. As many as 20 recording machines might be set up in one small room. Each machine had an enormous horn pointed at the spot where the singer was to stand. When everything was ready, the machines were started and the singer, taking a deep breath, would sing into

could figure out how to make multiple copies of a cylinder. Each one had to be an original recording. Then along came a man named Emile Berliner.

Like Tainter and Bell, Berliner had been working for several years to improve Edison's original invention. But he had some original ideas of his own as to how it could

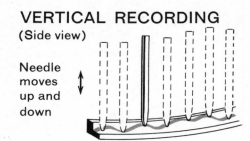

VERTICAL RECORDING
(Side view)

Needle moves up and down

LATERAL RECORDING
(Top view)

Needle moves from side to side

The two basic methods of cutting a record

be done. One of these ideas was for a new kind of record—not a cylinder, but a flat disk. On this disk the grooves containing the vibrations cut by the recording needle would spiral in from the edge of the record toward the center, just as they do on records you buy today.

Another of Berliner's ideas had to do with the way in which the record grooves were cut. In recording on a cylinder, the needle vibrated up and down, cutting more deeply into the wax in some places than in others. For this reason, this type of record was called a "hill and dale" or *vertical recording*. The drawing above shows what this kind of groove looked like. Berliner, however, built a recording machine in which the needle vibrated from side to side. The record groove was the same depth from beginning to end, but it wavered as shown in the drawing. This was called *lateral recording*.

Berliner's ideas were good ones. Lateral recordings gave a much better tone quality than the vertically recorded cylinders. Furthermore, when a cylinder was played back on a phonograph, the mechanism had not only to make the cylinder revolve but also to move the needle steadily along its surface. On a disk record, however, the playback needle would follow the spiral groove by itself. Thus the machinery could be much simpler.

The greatest advantage of the disk over the cylinder, however, was that a disk could be much more easily duplicated. Berliner himself realized this at once; but it took several more years of hard work, and many discouraging failures, before he developed a successful way of doing it. His method was as follows.

First, an original or *master recording* was made. This disk was then coated, by an electrical and chemical process, with a very thin sheet of copper mixed with nickel. When it was pulled away from the original recording, this metal sheet formed an exact negative, or reverse, of the original. Instead of grooves, it had ridges standing out from its surface. Then, after the negative had been stiffened and strengthened by adding more metal to the back, it could be used to stamp out duplicates of the original by the hundreds. The

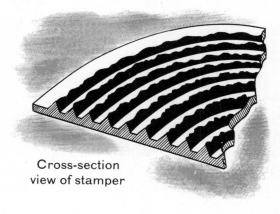

Cross-section view of stamper

material from which the duplicates were stamped was a *thermoplastic*—a material that became soft when heated and turned hard again when cool.

Eventually Edison, himself, switched to disk records, but his company continued to use the vertical recording method. Edison worked out improvements in this method until the tone quality of his records was as good as any on the market. The Edison Phonograph became the "Cadillac" of the industry. It was large, expensive, and beautifully made. It was also the first to use a diamond-tipped needle which, the company claimed, never had to be changed.

Only Edison records, however, could be played on an Edison Phonograph. As a result, the Edison Company eventually lost out in the race for popularity. Berliner's lateral recording remains today as the basic process of the recording industry.

Power from a clockwork motor

One more thing was needed to make the talking machine a success—a motor to run it. This may not seem like much of a problem, but in those days electricity had not yet come into common use. The only answer seemed to be a clockwork motor, but it was very difficult to build a motor that would not slow down as the spring gradually unwound.

The problem was solved by a mechanic who worked for a company which made clockwork sewing machine motors. This man, Eldridge Johnson, designed and built a clockwork motor fitted with a device called a *governor*. The governor controlled the speed of the motor and made it run evenly until the spring was almost unwound. The machine still had to be cranked, to wind the spring, before each record was played. But no one minded that and it was many years before electrically driven phonographs came into widespread use.

Two famous names

Eldridge Johnson came to Emile Berliner with his new phonograph motor and the two men went into business together. A factory was built in Camden, New Jersey, to manufacture phonographs using Johnson's motor and playing records made by Berliner's methods. The organization was named the Victor Talking Machine Company and it made Johnson a millionaire.

Anyone who has ever handled phonograph records is familiar with the little picture which appears on so many labels. It shows a small black and white dog sitting, with his head attentively cocked, listening to a large horn mounted on a small box. Underneath appear the words, "His Master's Voice." The phonograph has changed greatly throughout the years, but this drawing has not. It has become one of the most famous trademarks in the world.

For many years the Victor Talking Machine Company was the leader in its field. Its products were sold so widely that the word "Victrola" became a noun commonly used as the name of any record-playing machine whether it was built by Victor or not. Today, however, it has been displaced by the word phonograph, Edison's name for his original machine. Berliner's original trade-name was "Gramophone," and this word is now commonly used in England instead of the word phonograph.

About 1893 the Columbia Graphophone Company was formed. For several years this company manufactured cylinder records for the early types of players. Later, when the company switched to the disk type of record, the word Graphophone was dropped from the name, but the "Columbia Graphophone Company" still exists in England. Today, Columbia is one of the two largest record-makers in the United States.

Beginning the Big Business of Home Entertainment

As you have read, several improvements on Edison's original idea were necessary before the phonograph could become really successful. By 1900 these basic improvements had all been made. Tainter and Bell had invented the method of recording on hard wax, interchangeable cylinders. Berliner had invented the easily-copied disk record with lateral recording. And Johnson had perfected the clock-work motor. But it was still not possible to manufacture and sell a phonograph and records using all of these improvements.

One more hurdle

The trouble was that each inventor, as soon as he had worked out an improved way of making or playing records, at once patented his ideas. And no one company owned all the patents.

Berliner, for example, had the best system of making records—the flat disk with the lateral groove from which thousands of duplicates could be stamped. But his original, or master, recordings could not be cut in hard wax. The Graphophone Company owned that patent.

Berliner had therefore developed a system of etching the spiral groove into a zinc disk with acid. This master recording was then used to make the negative from which the duplicates were stamped. The system worked, but the grooves etched into the zinc master were rough and produced a very noisy record.

The system of cutting the original recording in hard wax produced a much quieter record. But the Graphophone Company could not use disk records. Berliner owned that patent. And so it went. All the necessary inventions had been made, but no one man or company had the right to use them all. What to do?

The sensible thing to do, was for everyone to get together and reach an agreement to help each other. And that is what did happen. In 1902 the various companies agreed to place their patents in a "pool." This meant that anyone who wanted to build phonographs or make records could use any system he liked.

As a result of this agreement, most of the companies which had been making cylinder records at once switched to disks. Berliner began cutting his masters in wax. The clock-work motor came into general use. The phonograph was on its way.

Opera in the living room

During the next few years the phonograph quickly became the most popular device yet invented for home entertainment. Many com-

172

An early phonograph

panies went into the business of building machines, hiring artists, and making records. Thousands of record dealers sprang up all over the country. Music stores had a new product to sell—one which brought them quick profits.

As the odd-looking machines, with their great flaring horns, appeared in thousands upon thousands of homes, music came in where it had never been known before. People everywhere, young and old, formed the habit of settling down of an evening to relax and listen to their records. Popular songs, recitations, arias from great operas, and violin or piano solos were favorites. Many of these people lived in small towns or on farms, far from the nearest concert hall. Most had never heard great music performed by a famous artist. The phonograph brought it to them.

During the early years of the twentieth century perhaps the most famous name in the world of music was Enrico Caruso. Caruso was the leading opera star of the day and, many people believe, the finest tenor who ever lived. The magic and power of his voice enthralled all who heard it. From the beginning, Caruso was interested in the phonograph and understood its possibilities. He was among the first of the great artists to record his voice and soon his records were being sold by the hundreds of thousands.

The fame of Caruso and the excitement of being able to hear him sing in one's own living room did much to increase the sale of phonographs and records. Other famous singers soon followed Caruso's example and Paderewski, the pianist, and Kreisler, the violinist, also made records.

Faults of the acoustical system

The system of recording invented by Edison and improved by Berliner and others was called the *acoustical* system. The sound waves created by the artist's voice or his instrument provided all the energy to move the needle which cut the record grooves. There was no way of *amplifying* or increasing this energy and much of it was lost in cutting the groove. Again, in playing a record, there was no way of amplifying the energy of the vibrating needle and diaphragm. The sound, even when concentrated and directed by the phonograph horn, was faint indeed.

The system was fairly well suited to recording vocal music. A singer could place his head almost within the mouth of the recording machine's horn. Then, especially if his voice had the power of a Caruso, his song would be recorded loudly and distinctly enough to reproduce fairly well. A piano, however, could not be placed close enough to the horn to record well. And a violin did not produce a powerful enough sound.

For many years it was impossible to record a large orchestra or band by means of the acoustical system. The single horn of the recording machine, no matter how big, could not possibly pick up all the many sounds of a large group of instruments. What came out when such a recording was tried was a hopeless jumble of sound.

Smaller groups, sometimes using specially designed instruments, could be grouped closely around the horn. Such groups were often used for accompaniment and provided a rhythmic, if not very musical, background for a singer.

The phonograph grows up

Between 1900 and 1920 great changes took place in both phonographs and records. The most obvious changes were in the phonograph itself. The little box grew in size until it became a large floor cabinet. The horn disappeared inside the cabinet, and the whole machine became an imposing and often beautiful piece of furniture.

Various minor improvements were made in methods of recording and in the phonograph sound system itself. The system as a whole was still the acoustical system, however, and the voice of even the largest cabinet phonograph was weak and thin at best. Diamond or sapphire needles were rare in those days and most records were played by steel needles which had to be thrown away after one or two playings. The user could choose between a "loud" needle and a "soft" needle. The latter was thinner than the loud needle and produced a somewhat sweeter tone. Some people preferred fiber needles which could be sharpened after each playing and used again. Even when a loud needle was used and the cabinet doors were wide open, one of these machines would scarcely disturb one's neighbor—or even a person in the next room!

By 1920, however, the phonograph and record industry had unquestionably become a big business. Millions of records had been sold. Nearly all of the famous artists of the day were at last ready to admit that this was no longer a toy. Much as they might disapprove of its sound quality, they knew that records were here to stay and joined the parade to the recording studios. Even small bands and orchestras were now being recorded with fairly satisfactory results.

Then, in a very short time, everything changed and the record industry was in deep trouble. A new form of home entertainment —radio—was sweeping the country.

A serious rival

On October 27, 1920, station KDKA in Pittsburgh was licensed by the government to make regular radio broadcasts. On November 2, a few listeners who had been experimenting with home-built receivers, heard KDKA broadcast the results of the presidential election. This date marked the beginning of a great new entertainment industry.

In the same year, station WWJ in Detroit also began sending programs over the air and hundreds of other stations soon followed. In 1922 a real estate dealer in Jackson Heights, New York, paid to have his advertisement read over the radio, and commercial broadcasting had begun. In 1926 the National Broadcasting Company was formed, linking together a number of stations. Now a single broadcast could be heard by listeners all across the nation.

Music in the air – a new idea

The early radio broadcasts were mainly records, with occasional "live" programs, and some news events. The listeners had to use head phones and properly adjust three or more dials on the receiving set in order to "bring in" a program. Most owners of early radios were not so much interested in what they heard as in where it came from. The idea was to see how many distant stations could be received and their dial settings noted in a "log." It was a fascinating game—one which kept many listeners at their dials into the early morning hours.

The quality of radio broadcasts and radio receivers rapidly improved. Thousands of sets were sold. And, in homes everywhere, the phonograph was pushed off into a corner or carried to the attic to gather dust. Radio was the new "wonder of the age" and record sales dropped.

Electrical Recording Saves the Day

Strangely enough, the very invention that made the phonograph seem old-fashioned eventually saved it. The principles of electricity that made possible radio broadcasting and receiving were soon applied to the making and playing of records. Electrical recording replaced the old acoustical system and gave the phonograph a new voice of amazing beauty and power.

Sound on a current of electricity

The drawing on this page illustrates, in a very simple way, how a record is made by electricity and played on an electrical pho-

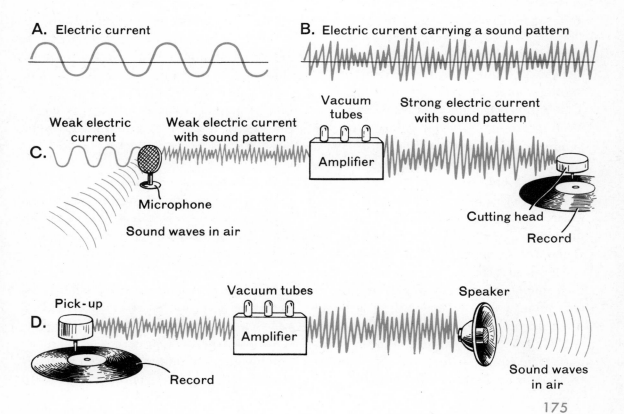

A. Electric current

B. Electric current carrying a sound pattern

C. Weak electric current — Weak electric current with sound pattern — Microphone — Sound waves in air — Vacuum tubes — Amplifier — Strong electric current with sound pattern — Cutting head — Record

D. Pick-up — Record — Vacuum tubes — Amplifier — Speaker — Sound waves in air

nograph. In this drawing you see three of the basic inventions which make the modern phonograph as well as the modern radio possible. These are the *microphone,* the *vacuum tube,* and the *loudspeaker.*

The microphone is an electrical device which changes sound waves in the air to electrical waves traveling through a wire. To understand exactly how it does this requires considerable knowledge of electricity, but there is an easy way to picture it to yourself.

Think of a microphone standing in an empty room. A weak current of electricity is passing through the microphone. Alternating current, or AC, such as is used in most homes, can be thought of as traveling through a wire in waves. As long as they are undisturbed, these waves are smooth and even in shape as Diagram A.

Now a violinist walks into the room and begins to play. As the sound waves strike the microphone they cause a diaphragm to vibrate, as in the old style recording machine. This diaphragm, however, is not connected to a needle. Instead, it is connected to an electrical circuit in such a way that its vibration changes the *resistance* of that circuit. That is, it becomes more, or less, easy for the electric current to flow through the wires, depending on how the diaphragm moves. As a result, the electrical waves lose their smooth, even shape and become jagged and uneven, as shown in Diagram B. The "wiggles" match exactly the vibrations of the diaphragm and the current now carries the pattern of the sound waves from the violin.

The electric current which comes from the microphone is a very weak current. So it is fed into a vacuum tube amplifier, as shown in Diagram C.

The vacuum tube was one of the most important inventions in the whole field of electricity. It is the heart of radio, television, and many other electrical wonders that we take for granted today. It can do many things, but its most important job is to use a very weak current to control a much stronger one. In doing this the pattern of the weak current is transferred to the strong current.

So, when the weak current from the microphone is fed into a vacuum tube amplifier, the amplifier produces a current that may be many thousands of times stronger. But this strong current carries exactly the same sound pattern as the weak current. We say that the weak current has been amplified.

The amplified current is then passed through wires to the *cutting head* of the recording machine. This is a device which, by means of a magnet, transforms the electrical waves to vibrations in a needle, or *stylus,* as it is now called. This stylus cuts the sound pattern into the record grooves.

To play a record, the electric phonograph simply reverses the recording process, as shown in Diagram D. The record grooves cause the stylus to vibrate. These vibrations are changed into a weak electric current, carrying the sound pattern. This weak current is then amplified and used to drive a loudspeaker. The speaker, in turn, changes the electrical waves to sound waves in the air.

A new world of recorded sound

Electrical recording brought about a great revolution in the record business. Nearly all the limits of the old acoustical system were removed and fascinating new possibilities were opened up.

First, the microphone made possible many new types of recording. The microphone is a very sensitive instrument. It can pick up the merest whisper in a far corner of the room. On the other hand, it can handle extremely loud sound. It is easily portable and can be taken anywhere. As a result, the electrical system made possible for the first time truly successful recording of large bands, symphony orchestras, and operas. The microphone clearly picked up the separate sounds of all the many instruments and faithfully transformed them into electrical waves. The whole world of sound was now opened up to the recording engineers.

Second, the vacuum tube amplifier made it possible to record the complex sounds picked up by the microphone with new realism. This was especially true of musical instruments. For the first time it was possible to tell a violin from a cello, a trumpet from a trombone. But the quality was improved most of all in the bass tones. The tympani, the bass viol, the low notes on the piano—all came through with breathtaking power and realism.

Third, the amplifier used in the electric phonograph made it possible to control the volume of sound. It could be turned low, for late evening listening, or up to fill a hall with music for dancing. Edison's invention had become a far richer and more flexible instrument for home entertainment than ever before.

More improvements

By 1926 electrical recording was firmly established, and the record companies were exploring new fields of music to be put on disks. Recordings of full-length symphonies, concertos, and operas became very popular. These longer works could not, of course, be put on a single record. The standard record size for such works was then, as now, 12 inches in diameter. At the standard speed of 78 revolutions per minute, such a record would play for about 4 minutes per side. It took about five records to record a full symphony and twice as many for an opera.

The sound of the new recordings was thrilling. But it was an inconvenience to have to get up every 4 minutes to change the record, to say nothing of the disconcerting breaks in the flow of the music. The engineers went to work to solve this problem and in the early 1930's the automatic record changer was introduced. Soon all but the smallest portable phonographs were equipped with changers. These clever machines ended the inconvenience of having to get out of one's chair every few minutes. They were fine for dance music, songs, or other short numbers. But there were still those annoying breaks in the middle of a symphony while the machine clanked into action and dropped another record into place.

Then, in 1948, Columbia engineers introduced the Long Playing, or Microgroove record. This new kind of record was as revolutionary an improvement as electrical recording itself. It had three great advantages over the older records.

First, the "LP's," as they soon came to be called, are as their name tells us "long playing." Turning at a speed of $33\frac{1}{3}$ revolutions per minute, and having much narrower grooves much closer together, they will hold as much as 30 minutes of music on each side. A full symphony can be recorded on a single record.

Second, the quality of sound produced by the new process is far better than most of the older records. There is as much difference between an LP of today and an electrical recording of 1940 as there was between that record and an ancient acoustical recording.

Third, the LP's are much "quieter" records. They are made from a new kind of plastic which provides extremely smooth grooves. As a result, the annoying scratches and "hiss" of the older records are almost entirely gone. There is no sound but the music itself.

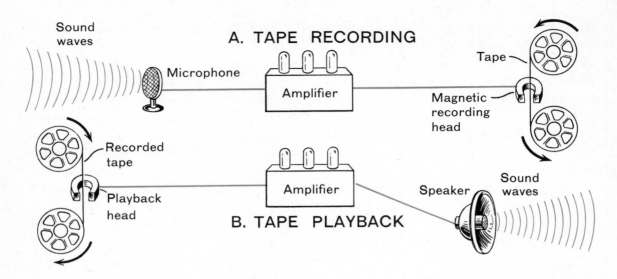

A. TAPE RECORDING

Sound waves

Microphone

Amplifier

Tape

Magnetic recording head

Recorded tape

Playback head

Amplifier

Speaker

Sound waves

B. TAPE PLAYBACK

Of course, there was one great drawback which some people thought would prevent the LP's from becoming a success. They could not be played on the equipment that people already owned. A special "player" was required with a turntable that revolved at the new slow speed, and a special stylus for the narrower grooves. But the advantages of the new records were so obvious that people were willing to buy the special players. Soon all new phonographs were equipped to play both types of records, as well as 45 r.p.m. records which are now used mainly for popular songs and other shorter works. Within a few years the manufacture of the old-style 78's had almost ceased.

A new rival for records

At about the same time that LP records were being introduced, an interesting new method of recording sound was also suddenly becoming popular. This was tape recording.

Tape recording was developed by German scientists during World War II and was introduced in this country shortly after. This is a process based on rather complicated principles of magnetism and electricity. But the drawing on this page will give you a simple idea of how it works.

In tape recording, the weak current from a microphone is amplified, just as in the electrical recording of records. The amplified current, carrying the sound pattern, is then fed into a magnetic *recording head*, as shown in Diagram A, above. The tape is made of plastic, which has been coated with a thin film of iron particles. As the tape passes through the recording head, this film becomes magnetized in exactly the same pattern as that carried by the electric current from the amplifier.

To play back a recorded tape, the process is reversed. The tape passes through the *playback head*, which picks up the magnetic pattern from the tape and changes it into a weak electric current. This current is then amplified and fed into the speaker, as shown in Diagram B.

Portable tape recorders which could be taken anywhere soon became very popular. Family activities, as well as radio programs, could be recorded and played back immediately. Soon, too, many companies began selling "pre-recorded tapes." These were tape records of music which could be played on home players.

178

Tape recordings have two advantages over records. There is no "surface noise"—no scratch or hiss such as even the best LP's may develop. Also, there is very little wear. With care, a tape should last indefinitely.

So far, however, tapes are much more expensive than records, and they are not so easy to store and to play. It is doubtful that tapes will ever take the place of records. On the other hand, tape recording has come to play a very important part in the process of making records, as we shall see.

Making the Record You Buy Today

The record-making business today is a huge industry. Many millions of records are made and sold every year. And every one of those records is still made according to Edison's basic principle—sound waves causing a needle or stylus to vibrate as it cuts a groove in wax. The ways of doing this have changed greatly, however, as a visit to a recording studio will quickly show.

From "mike" to tape

A modern recording studio is a busy, noisy, and often confusing place. Workmen move around the room carrying microphones from which trail long lines of electric wires. Musicians stroll about, or sit tuning their instruments. Over there stands a singer, perhaps arguing with the leader of the orchestra about how a certain phrase should be played. In another room the recording engineers are checking their equipment, making sure that everything is ready.

Then, suddenly, quiet falls. Everyone is in his place, the microphones are properly adjusted, and the last violin is tuned. As the conductor raps with his baton and begins the introduction, the recording machine starts and the engineers lean intently over their dials and knobs.

But now something strange happens—at least it might well seem strange to an outsider. Before he is halfway through the song, the singer breaks off in the middle of a phrase and the orchestra stops playing. After a minute or two of lively discussion as to what went wrong, the song is begun again—

A modern recording session

179

but not from the beginning. The orchestra starts playing only a few bars before the place where the mistake occurred. This may happen several times before the song is finally completed. And all the while, the recording machine continues to run, faithfully recording the arguments of the musicians as well as the music.

How can this be? Until a few years ago a recording could not have been made in this way. Then, if a mistake occurred, the master record which was being cut had to be thrown away. A new record was put on the machine, and the artist had to start over from the beginning. The whole composition had to be performed perfectly from start to finish before the recording session was over. This is no longer necessary and the tape recorder is the answer.

In making a recording today, the master record is almost never made at the time of the actual performance. The music is first recorded on tape. Then, perhaps weeks or months later, the tape is run through a machine which changes its magnetic pattern to an electric current, amplifies it, and cuts the master record. But, before this is done, the tape has been edited.

Editing a tape

Perhaps you have seen someone who takes home movies edit his film—perhaps you have done it yourself. The parts of the film that did not turn out well are simply cut out and thrown away. Then the ends of the film are cemented together so that only the best parts of the movie remain.

A tape recording is edited in much the same way. Any parts that are not wanted, or are not perfect, can be cut out. Then the ends of the good part of the tape are spliced together. That is why the singer at the recording session did not have to go back to the beginning when he made a mistake. He simply began again a few bars before the mistake occurred, and the wrong note—as well as the conversation—was later removed when the tape was edited.

This use of tape in the making of records has several great advantages. Master records are expensive and, before the coming of tape, great numbers of them had to be thrown away at every recording session. Then again, an artist might get all the way through one side of a record with no errors. But he might feel that he had not given his best performance. Rather than throw away the master, however, he might let it go or the recording engineers might insist that it was "good enough." In this way, many inferior records were made.

Tape, however, is cheap. A singer, for example, can stop in the middle of a song, and repeat a single phrase a dozen times if he likes. Only the best will be used in the final recording. Thus it is much easier now to get top quality performances on records.

The advantages of tape are even greater, of course, when a long symphony or concerto is being recorded. Symphony orchestra conductors usually insist that their performance must be perfect right down to the last note. So, after such a session many thousands of feet of tape may be thrown away to get 100 feet of perfect music. But how much worse it would be if, just before the end of a 30-minute LP side, some second violinist played a sour note and the whole orchestra had to begin again from the beginning. That is what often happened before tape was used. It is no wonder then that recording sessions often produced as much bad temper as good music!

From master to "mother" to stamper

When the tape has been finally edited, the next step is to cut the master record. The machine which does this is much like the home playback machine shown in Diagram B on page 178. Instead of a speaker, however, it has an electric cutting head. When the amplified current, carrying the sound pattern, is fed into this head, the stylus vibrates and cuts the pattern into the record groove.

Wax is no longer used for the master record. Instead, these records are made of a hard but brittle material called lacquer. This is very similar to the fluid lacquer that is often used to give a protective coating to furniture.

When the master record has been cut, it is very carefully packed in a strong wooden box in such a way that nothing can touch its surface. It is then sent to the plating department. This is an evil-smelling room filled with large tanks of green, yellow, and orange liquids. Here the master, through a process using chemicals and electricity, is given an extremely thin coat of pure silver. This silver coating is then "backed up" with harder metals to give it strength. The result, when it is stripped away from the master, is a hard metal "negative" record, with ridges instead of grooves. Thus far the process is very similar to that invented by Emile Berliner.

This negative record could be used as a stamper to mold the records you buy in the store. However, in making it, the lacquer master is usually damaged and has to be thrown away. If the negative were used as a stamper, it would eventually wear out and there would be no way of replacing it.

The metal negative, therefore, in its turn goes through a plating process much like that given the original lacquer master. This produces a metal positive record—an exact duplicate in metal of the original. The "mother," as this positive record is called, can be played and sometimes is used for testing purposes. Its chief purpose, however, is to serve as the mold from which the actual stamper is made. The "mother" is always kept on file and, as the stampers wear out, new ones can be made as they are needed. The drawing below shows the steps in the process, from lacquer master to stamper.

Making the actual record

The final step in making the record you buy takes place in the stamping department. This is a large room containing rows of machines not unlike large and rather complicated waffle irons. Like an electric waffle iron, each record press has two round faces, hinged at the back, containing molds. Of course, these molds are not the familiar waffle iron grids. They are the record stampers with ridges instead of grooves. And, instead of being heated by electricity, the two halves of the stamper are heated by high pressure steam at a temperature of 300°.

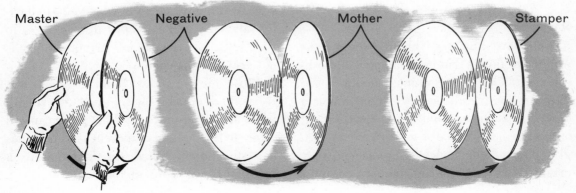

Master   Negative   Mother   Stamper

They can also be quickly cooled by cold water circulating through built-in pipes.

Beside each record press is a hot plate much like the one on which a short-order chef cooks your hamburger at the lunch counter. On the hot plate are several biscuit-shaped pieces of plastic. The heat has made them as soft as dough. Also near each press are two piles of record labels—one for each side of the record.

When everything is ready, the operator of the press quickly makes a "sandwich." First a label, face down. Then a biscuit of soft "dough." Then another label on top, face up. As the jaws of the press close, hot steam hisses through each mould and the plastic dough becomes as soft as butter. The pressure of the closing jaws forces it into each tiny record groove. Then comes the ice-cold water, suddenly cooling the plastic. The jaws open and a shiny new record, complete with labels, is lifted out. The rough edges are then trimmed off by a machine something like an electric can opener.

The complicated process is now finished. The music that a microphone "heard" in some distant studio is now stored, with wonderful accuracy, in the tiny record grooves. Each record is inspected by trained workers for any visible defects. A certain number out of each lot are actually played. Then the perfect records are put in their albums and shipped to your music store, ready to give you many hours of entertainment.

Stereophonic recording

You have now read about some of the wonderful things that have happened to Edison's scratchy little talking machine. And they are wonderful. Even when one knows a great deal about both music and electricity, it is hard to believe that a modern LP record, played on a modern phonograph is not partly magic. How can the enormously complex sound of a great orchestra be imprisoned in the wiggles of a tiny record groove? How can these wiggles re-create this sound with such realism? But we all know that it is not magic. It really happens. And even more wonderful things are possible.

One of those wonders is already here. Beginning in the summer of 1958, no one interested in recorded music could fail to realize that something new was happening. Across the country newspaper and magazine advertisements were shouting the word *stereo*. Stereo records. Stereo phonographs.

What is stereo? The word is a contraction of *stereophonic* which means, literally, "solid sound," or sound having three dimensions.

Now of course sound does not have dimensions—length, breadth, and depth—that you can actually measure. But you can hear them. If you sit in a concert hall, listening to an orchestra, you can close your eyes and still tell which sounds are coming from the right of the stage and which are coming from the left. You can tell which instruments are closest to you and which are farther away.

You can do this because you hear with two ears, not one. Each ear hears the sound in a slightly different way and your brain blends the two sound patterns in such a way as to give you a feeling of direction and depth in the music. In exactly the same way, your eyes, because they are separated, see two slightly different views of what you are looking at. This makes it possible for you to "see" depth—you can tell that one object is closer to you than another.

Close one eye and what you see looks flat. It has no depth. Likewise, in a concert hall, put a finger in one ear. What you hear will immediately sound different. It becomes flat—the sound all seems to come from nearly the same point on the stage.

Until the coming of stereo, the phonograph sounded the same way—as though you were listening to music with one ear closed. It produced wonderfully fine sound, but it was flat. You could easily tell this by listening to music played "live" in a concert hall and then comparing it with even the best recording.

The reason for this is easy to understand. The recording machine "listens" with only one ear. Even if there are two or more microphones, the current from each is fed through a single amplifier and becomes a single pattern of sound on the tape. Engineers call this a single sound channel. The standard phonograph, which plays the record made from this tape, also has a single sound channel. Although it may have more than one speaker, each plays exactly *the same* sound. You are still listening with only one ear.

What happens in stereo? The drawing on this page will help you to understand.

Suppose two microphones are set up in front of an orchestra, one to the right and one to the left. You can see that the sound pattern picked up by each will be slightly different. Now suppose that the current, or *output*, of each microphone is fed to a *separate* amplifier. Each amplifier, in turn, feeds a separate recording head and two sound patterns, side by side, are recorded on the tape. Each *sound track*, as they are called, is the image of what one of the microphones picked up. Each is slightly different from the other.

Now suppose that the tape playback machine also has two heads so that it can play both sound tracks at once. Each track is amplified separately and fed into a separate speaker. We now have a *two-channel* sound system—stereo.

Stereo first became popular on tape, be-

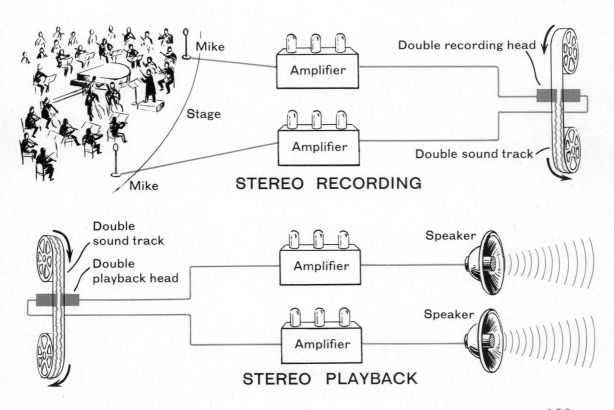

Mike
Amplifier
Stage
Amplifier
Mike
Double recording head
Double sound track
STEREO RECORDING

Double sound track
Double playback head
Amplifier
Amplifier
Speaker
Speaker
STEREO PLAYBACK

cause it was easy to record and play back two sound channels on a single tape. But soon engineers developed a way of recording two channels—two different sets of wiggles—in a single record groove. This sounds impossible? No more impossible than the original LP seemed at the time.

To play the new stereo disks, a phonograph must have a special pickup, two amplifiers, and two speakers. The results are better, also, if one of the speakers is in a separate cabinet which can be placed on the other side of the room.

This equipment is expensive, of course. But there seems to be little doubt that stereo records eventually will outsell all other kinds. This is so because of the wonderful new realism that stereo brings to recorded music. It is impossible to describe in words the breath-taking effect of hearing "with two ears" a full orchestra in your own home.

New things to come

Stereo is the latest and perhaps the greatest wonder in the story of the phonograph. But it is not the last. We cannot tell what more improvements are to come. But we can be sure of one thing. As long as musicians and scientists continue to work together to bring better music to everyone, wonders will not cease.

For He's a Jolly Good Fellow—F $\frac{6}{8}$

```
         F              Bb F
For / he's a jolly good fellow,
     C7            F
For he's a jolly good fellow,
     F              Bb
For he's a jolly good fellow,
     F       C7   F
Which nobody can deny!
     F       Bb    F
Which nobody can deny,
     F       Bb    F
Which nobody can deny,
     F              Bb F
For he's a jolly good fellow,
     C7            F
For he's a jolly good fellow,
     F              Bb
For he's a jolly good fellow,
         F    C7   F
Which nobody can deny!
```

Auld Lang Syne—F $\frac{4}{4}$

```
    C7        F           C7
1. Should / auld acquaintance be forgot,
         F         Bb
And never bro't to mind?
         F             C7
Should auld acquaintance be forgot,
a min. d min. Bb  C7  F
And   days  of auld lang syne?

     Bb  F     C7
Ref: For auld lang syne, my dear,
     C7 F      Bb
For auld lang syne;
          F         C7
We'll tak' a cup o' kindness yet
A7  d min. Bb C7 F
For auld   lang  syne.

    C7    F              C7
2. And here's a hand, my trusty frien',
         F         Bb
And gie's a hand o' thine;
         F        C7
We'll tak' a cup o' kindness yet,
a min. d min. Bb C7 F
For    auld   lang  syne.
```

The More We Get Together—F $\frac{3}{4}$

```
        F                    C7          F
The / more we get together, together, together,
        F                    C7          F
The more we get together, the happier are we.
         C7            F
And your friends are my friends,
         C7          F
And my friends are your friends;
        F                    C7          F
The more we get together, the happier are we.
```

Vive l'Amour—C $\frac{6}{8}$

```
                    C
1. Come, / every good fellow, and join in the song,
   C     G7    C
Vive la compagnie!
                    C
A song for our school, make it lusty and strong,
   C     G7    C
Vive la compagnie!

        C          F
Ref: Vive la, vive la, vive l'amour,
     G7            C
Vive la, vive la, vive l'amour,
     C    C7   d min. D7
Vive l'amour, vive l'amour,
     G7            C
Vive la compagnie!

                    C
2. The song that we sing will be merry and gay,
   C     G7    C
Vive la compagnie!
                    C
We'll laugh at our troubles and toss them away,
   C     G7    C
Vive la compagnie!
```

MacDonald's Farm—G $\frac{2}{4}$

G   C G   D₇ G
Old MacDonald had a farm, ee-i, ee-i-o,
  G   C G   D₇ G
And on this farm he had a duck, ee-i, ee-i-o.
     G
With a quack, quack here and a quack, quack there,
G
Here a quack, there a quack,
G
Here and there a quack, quack,
G   C G   D₇ G
Old MacDonald had a farm, ee-i-ee-i-o.

The Little Brown Church
in the Vale—G $\frac{4}{4}$

     G C G   D₇
1. There's a / church in the valley by the wildwood,
   D₇   G
No lovelier place in the dale;
   C   G
No spot is so dear to my childhood
     D₇   G
As the little brown church in the vale.

     G
Ref: Oh, come, come, come, come,
   G C G   D₇
Come to the church in the wildwood,
   D₇   G
Oh, come to the church in the dale;
   C   G
No spot is so dear to my childhood
     D₇   G
As the little brown church in the vale.

    G C G   D₇
2. How sweet on a bright Sabbath morning
   D₇   G
To list to the clear ringing bell;
   C   G
Its tones so sweetly are calling,
   D₇   G
Oh, come to the church in the vale.

Clementine—F $\frac{3}{4}$

       F
1. In a / cavern by a canyon,
    F   C₇
Excavating for a mine,
    C₇   F
Dwelt a miner, forty-niner,
     C₇   F
And his daughter, Clementine.

       F
Ref: Oh, my darling, oh, my darling,
      F   C₇
Oh, my darling Clementine,
     C₇   F
Thou art lost and gone forever,
     C₇   F
Dreadful sorry, Clementine.

       F
2. Light she was and like a feather,
     F   C₇
And her shoes were number nine;
    C₇   F
Herring boxes without topses
    C₇   F
Sandals were for Clementine.

       F
3. Drove she ducklings to the water
    F   C₇
Every morning just at nine;
    C₇   F
Struck her foot against a splinter,
    C₇   F
Fell into the foaming brine.

       F
4. Rosy lips above the water
    F   C₇
Blowing bubbles mighty fine;
    C₇   F
But, alas! I was no swimmer,
    C₇   F
So I lost my Clementine.

       F
5. How I missed her! How I missed her!
    F   C₇
How I missed my Clementine;
    C₇   F
'Til I kissed her little sister,
    C₇   F
Then forgot my Clementine.

Home on the Range—G $^6_8$

           G   C
1. Oh, / give me a home where the buffalo roam,
         G   A₇   D₇
Where the deer and the antelope play,
        G   C
Where seldom is heard a discouraging word,
        G   D₇   G
And the skies are not cloudy all day.

G   D₇   G
Ref: Home, home on the range,
             G   A₇   D₇
Where the deer and the antelope play,
        G   C
Where seldom is heard a discouraging word,
        G   D₇   G
And the skies are not cloudy all day.

           G   C
2. Where the air is so pure, and the zephyrs so free,
        G   A₇   D₇
The breezes so balmy and light,
        G   C
That I would not exchange my home on the range
        G   D₇   G
For all of the cities so bright.

          G   C
3. How often at night when the heavens are bright
        G   A₇   D₇
With the lights from the glittering stars,
        G   C
Have I stood there amazed and asked as I gazed,
        G   D₇   G
If their glory exceeds that of ours.

          G   C
4. Oh, give me a land where the bright diamond sand
        G   A₇   D₇
Flows leisurely down the stream;
        G   C
Where the graceful white swan goes gliding along
        G   D₇   G
Like a maid in a heavenly dream.

My Bonnie—G $^3_4$

          G   C   G
1. My / Bonnie lies over the ocean,
        G   A₇   D₇
My Bonnie lies over the sea,
        G   C   G
My Bonnie lies over the ocean,
       a min.   D₇   G
Oh, bring back my Bonnie to me.

        G   C
Ref: Bring back, bring back,
       D₇   G
Bring back my Bonnie to me, to me;
       G   C   A₇
Bring back, bring back,
       D₇   G
Oh, bring back my Bonnie to me.

        G   C   G
2. Oh, blow, ye winds, over the ocean,
        G   A₇   D₇
And blow, ye winds, over the sea,·
        G   C   G
Oh, blow, ye winds, over the ocean,
       a min.   D₇   G
And bring back my Bonnie to me.

        G   C   G
3. The winds have blown over the ocean,
        G   A₇   D₇
The winds have blown over the sea,
        G   C   G
The winds have blown over the ocean,
       a min.   D₇   G
And brought back my Bonnie to me.

Polly Wolly Doodle—F 4/4

1. Oh, I / went down South for to see my Sal,   *(F)*

Sing Polly wolly doodle all the day;   *(F ... C7)*

My Sal, she is a spunky gal,   *(C7)*

Sing Polly wolly doodle all the day.   *(C7 ... F)*

Ref: Fare thee well, fare thee well,   *(F ... F)*

Fare thee well, my fairy fay;   *(F ... C7)*

For I'm goin' to Louisiana for to see my Susyanna,   *(C7)*

Sing Polly wolly doodle all the day.   *(C7 ... F)*

2. Oh, my Sal, she is a maiden fair,   *(F)*

Sing Polly wolly doodle all the day;   *(F ... C7)*

With curly eyes and laughing hair,   *(C7)*

Sing Polly wolly doodle all the day.   *(C7 ... F)*

3. A grass hopper sittin' on a railroad track,   *(F)*

Sing Polly wolly doodle all the day;   *(F ... C7)*

A-pickin' his teeth with a carpet tack,   *(C7)*

Sing Polly wolly doodle all the day.   *(C7 ... F)*

The Man on the Flying Trapeze—G 3/4

Ref: He / floats through the air with the greatest of ease,   *(G ... a min.)*

That daring young man on the flying trapeze;   *(D7 ... G)*

His movements are graceful; all the girls he does please,   *(G ... a min.)*

And my love he has stolen away.   *(D7 ... G)*

Shoo, Fly, Don't Bother Me—G 2/4

Ref: Shoo, fly, don't bother me!   *(G ... D7)*

Shoo, fly, don't bother me!   *(D7 ... G)*

Shoo, fly, don't bother me!   *(G ... D7)*

I belong to somebody.   *(D7 ... G D7 G)*

I feel, I feel, I feel,   *(G)*

I feel like a morning star,   *(G ... D7)*

I feel, I feel, I feel,   *(D7)*

I feel like a morning star.   *(D7 ... G)*

So shoo, fly, don't bother me!   *(D7 G ... D7)*

Shoo, fly, don't bother me!   *(D7 ... G)*

Shoo, fly, don't bother me!   *(G ... D7)*

I belong to somebody.   *(D7 ... G D7 G)*

Alouette—F 4/4

Ref: Alouette, gentille Alouette,   *(F ... C7 ... F)*

Alouette, je te plumerai.   *(F ... C7 ... F)*

1. Je te plumerai la tête,   *(F)*

Je te plumerai la tête,   *(C7 ... F)*

Et la tête, et la tête.   *(C)*

Alouette, Alouette. Oh!   *(C ... C7)*

Alouette, gentille Alouette,   *(F ... C7 ... F)*

Alouette, je te plumerai.   *(F ... C7 ... F)*

2. Le bec   4. Le dos

3. Le nez   5. Les pattes

6. Le cou

Deck the Hall—F $\frac{4}{4}$

    F
1. Deck the hall with boughs of holly,
    C₇   F   C₇F
    Fa la la la la, la la la la,
    F
    'Tis the season to be jolly,
    C₇   F   C₇F
    Fa la la la la, la la la la;
    C₇   F   C₇
    Don we now our gay apparel,
    F   C G₇C-C₇
    Fa la la la la la la la la,
    F
    Troll the ancient Yuletide carol,
    Bb   F   C₇F
    Fa la la la la, la la la la!

    F
2. See the blazing Yule before us,
    C₇   F   C₇F
    Fa la la la la, la la la la,
    F
    Strike the harp and join the chorus,
    C₇   F   C₇F
    Fa la la la la, la la la la;
    C₇   F   C₇
    Follow me in merry measure,
    F   C G₇C-C₇
    Fa la la la la la la la la,
    F
    While I tell of Yuletide treasure,
    Bb   F   C₇F
    Fa la la la la, la la la la!

    F
3. Fast away the old year passes,
    C₇   F   C₇F
    Fa la la la la, la la la la,
    F
    Hail the new, ye lads and lasses,
    C₇   F   C₇F
    Fa la la la la, la la la la;
    C₇   F   C₇
    Sing we joyous all together,
    F   C G₇C-C₇
    Fa la la la la la la la la,
    F
    Heedless of the wind and weather,
    Bb   F   C₇F
    Fa la la la la, la la la la!

The First Noël—C $\frac{3}{4}$

    C   C a min.G d min. C F C
1. The / first No - ël the   angel did say,
    F   C   F   C   G₇C   G₇ C
    Was to certain poor shepherds in fields as they lay,
    G₇C a min.G d min.C   F   C
    In fields where they lay, keeping their sheep,
    F   C   G₇ C G₇C
    On a cold winter's night that was so deep.

        G₇C a min.G C F   C
Ref: Noël, No - ël, Noël, Noël
    a min. F C   G₇C G₇C
    Born is the King of Is- ra- el.

        G₇   C a min.G d min.C F C
2. They looked   up and   saw a star
    F   C F C G₇C G₇ C
    Shining in the East beyond them far,
    G₇   C a min.G d min.C   F   C
    And to the   earth it   gave great light,
    F C   G₇ C G₇C
    And so it continued both day and night.

Joy to the World—C $\frac{2}{4}$

    C   F C G₇C
1. Joy to the world! The Lord is come;
    F   G₇   C
    Let earth receive her King;
    C
    Let ev'ry heart prepare Him room,
    C
    And heav'n and nature sing,
    G₇
    And heav'n and nature sing,
    C   F C d min.C G₇ C
    And heav'n, and heav'n and nature sing.

    C   F C G₇ C
2. He rules the world with truth and grace,
    F   G₇   C
    And makes the nations prove
    C
    The glories of His righteousness,
    C
    And wonders of His love,
    G₇
    And wonders of His love,
    C F   C d min.C G₇ C
    And wonders, wonders of His love.

I've Been Working on the Railroad—F $\frac{4}{4}$ ($\frac{2}{4}$)

F
I've been workin' on the railroad

Bb   F
All the livelong day;

F
I've been workin' on the railroad,

   G7   C7
To pass the time away.

C7   F
Don't you hear the whistle blowin'?

Bb   A7
Rise up so early in the morn.

Bb   F   G7
Don't you hear the captain shoutin',

 F   C7   F
"Dinah, blow your horn"?

F   Bb   g min.
Dinah, won't you blow, Dinah, won't you blow,

C7   F
Dinah, won't you blow your horn, your horn;

F   Bb   G7
Dinah, won't you blow, Dinah, won't you blow,

C7   F
Dinah, won't you blow your horn?

F
Someone's in the kitchen with Dinah,

F   C7
Someone's in the kitchen, I know,

F   Bb
Someone's in the kitchen with Dinah,

F   C7   F
Strummin' on the old banjo.

F
Fee, fi, fiddle-ee-i-o,

F   C7
Fee, fi, fiddle-ee-i-o,

F   Bb
Fee, fi, fiddle-ee-i-o,

F   C7   F
Strummin' on the old banjo.

Red River Valley—G $\frac{4}{4}$

              G   C
1. From this / valley they say you are going;

          G   D7
We will miss your bright eyes and sweet smile,

          G   C
For they say you are taking the sunshine

          G   D7   G
That brightens our pathway awhile.

              G   C
Ref: Come and sit by my side if you love me,

          G   D7
Do not hasten to bid me adieu;

          G   C
But remember the Red River Valley

          G   D7   G
And the girl that has loved you so true.

              G   C
2. Won't you think of the valley you're leaving?

          G   D7
Oh, how lonely, how sad it will be!

          G   C
Oh, think of the fond heart you're breaking,

          G   D7   G
And the grief you are causing to me.

Good Night, Ladies—G $\frac{4}{4}$

    G
1. Good night, ladies!

    G   D7
Good night, ladies!

    G   C
Good night, ladies!

       G   D7   G
We're going to leave you now.

          G
Ref: Merrily we roll along,

    D7   G
Roll along, roll along,

    G
Merrily we roll along,

    D7   G
O'er the deep blue sea.

2. Farewell, ladies!

3. Sweet dreams, ladies!

CLASSIFIED INDEX

Man on the Flying Trapeze, The
  (*text only*), 188
Marines' Hymn, The, 104
On Sunday Afternoon, 39
Paddy Works on the Railroad, 23
Red River Valley (*text only*), 190

Four Chords
All Through the Night, 61
Amazing Grace, 73
Amsterdam, 18
Blow, Ye Winds, 20
Dear Lahyotte, 22

Dixie, 130
Farmer's Boy, The, 47
Home on.the Range (*text only*), 187
Jingle Bells, 134
John Grumlie, 124
Joy to the World (*text only*), 189
Santa Lucia, 44

Five Chords
Deck the Hall (*text only*), 189
I Found a Horseshoe, 120
I Know an Old Lady, 118
My Bonnie (*text only*), 187

Six Chords
Auld Lang Syne (*text only*), 185
First Noël, The (*text only*), 189
Good Friends, Good Fellow!, 37
Hatikvah, 56
I've Been Working on the Railroad
  (*text only*), 190
Pretty Saro, 13
Semper Paratus, 106
Vive l'Amour (*text only*), 185

Nine Chords
Let Us Break Bread Together, 25

INDEX TO SONGS

INDEX TO INSTRUMENTAL THEMES

56 7 8 9 10 11 12 JCP 67 66 65 64 63 62 61

DATE DUE

GAYLORD			PRINTED IN U.S.A.

PLASTIC BO...
REMAIN IN POCKET AT
TIMES. A FEE WILL BE
CHARGED IF BADGE I...

PIANO KEYBOARD